Copyright © Kari Nars 2009
Cover art: OpalWorks Co. Ltd.
Photo credits: Corbis: 102, 129, 153, 162, 168; Topfoto: 77, 193; STT Lehtikuva: 179; Wikipedia: 113; Wikimedia Commons: 91
English edition published by agreement with Tammi Publishers & Elina Ahlback Literary Agency, Helsinki, Finland. This work has been published with the financial assistance of FILI – Finnish Literature Exchange.

This edition is published in 2011 by Marshall Cavendish Business
An imprint of Marshall Cavendish International

PO Box 65829
London EC1P 1NY
United Kingdom
info@marshallcavendish.co.uk
and

1 New Industrial Road, Singapore 536196
genrefsales@sg.marshallcavendish.com
www.marshallcavendish.com/genref

Other Marshall Cavendish offices: Marshall Cavendish International (Asia) Private Limited. 1 New Industrial Road, Singapore 536196 • Marshall Cavendish Corporation. 99 White Plains Road, Tarrytown NY 10591-9001, USA • Marshall Cavendish International (Thailand) Co Ltd. 253 Asoke, 12th Flr, Sukhumvit 21 Road, Klongtoey Nua, Wattana, Bangkok 10110, Thailand • Marshall Cavendish (Malaysia) Sdn Bhd. Times Subang, Lot 46, Subang Hi-Tech Industrial Park, Batu Tiga, 40000 Shah Alam, Selangor Darul Ehsan, Malaysia

Marshall Cavendish is a trademark of Times Publishing Limited

The right of Kari Nars to be identified as the author of this work has been asserted by him in accordance with the Copyright, Designs and Patents Act 1988.

A CIP record for this book is available from the British Library

ISBN 978-981-4328-06-7

Printed and bound in Great Britain by TJ International Limited, Padstow, Cornwall

KARI NARS

SWINDLING BILLIONS

AN EXTRAORDINARY HISTORY OF THE GREAT MONEY FRAUDSTERS

Marshall Cavendish
Business

To my dear family,
for putting up with the author
during the writing process.

CONTENTS

Introduction

This book offers a road map to the fascinating landscape of the world's most spectacular money swindles.

It promises the reader perfect hindsight. And also food for thought for malicious *schadenfreude* addicts.

The naked truth is that rich Western societies encourage values, attitudes and personality structures conducive to white-collar crime. In the words of Ian Taylor, the market economy promotes crime via

> "its magnification of a culture of Darwinian competition for status and resources and its encouragement of a level of consumption it cannot provide for everyone through legitimate channels".

In this environment swindlers have created tempting and often ingenious money-making traps, promising princely rewards to credulous people. The victims fall for the temptations offered in the hope of making what they regard as particularly well-deserved big money right away, now, immediately.

Heartless, conniving swindlers break the law because it is the easiest way for them to make a fast buck. Along with the desire for wealth goes the desire to prove themselves by winning in the competitive struggles that play such a prominent role in our economic systems. The winners are admired for their ability and drive.

Major crime has become one of the greatest public concerns of our time. Almost daily the mass media reports shocking murders, robberies and street crime. But our eyes are so focused on violent crimes that many financial swindles catch less attention.

The US Senate Judiciary Subcommittee estimated that in the 1970s, corporate crime – including swindles – had already cost the public a staggering US$500 billion to US$700 billion a year in today's money. At a time when the average take for a robbery was a paltry US$434.[1] The yearly losses from street crime were estimated at US$4 billion, only a fraction of the losses from corporate crime.

White-collar crime, such as swindles, always involves a violation of trust. The swindlers violate the trust put in them by their victims: investors, depositors, banks, company boards, fellow employees and the media. Because they attack the fundamental principles of Western societies – honesty, trust and transparency – swindlers undermine social mores and produce social disorganisation, while other crimes such as robbery or burglary have little effect on society morale or social institutions.

As an economist and banker, I have worked in the financial world for almost 50 years, at the IMF in Washington D.C., as long-time board chairman of the Council of Europe Development Bank in Paris, as a board member of the Nordic Investment Bank and of the EBRD in London, and as a director of the Bank of Finland and the Ministry of Finance. During this time, I have been perplexed to see how careless and unsuspecting many busy people are in personal money matters.

The book focuses on my special selection of the "Top 10" financial swindles. All of them are interesting, different, even staggering, and they concerned large numbers of people; they made headline news at the time and most of them were ingenious.

For the sake of readability, some cases that are difficult to describe in a simple way, such as the story of the junk bond king Michael Milken, and the insider trader Ivan Boesky, are not covered. Neither are the billion-dollar derivative trading losses caused by Nick Leeson in Barings Bank, or Jerome Kerviel in Société General.

I start with a general analysis of financial fraud: what kind of people were the swindlers, what were their thought processes, who are liable

[1] All dollars subsequently mentioned refer to US dollars, unless otherwise indicated.

to become such criminals, how do they design their criminal schemes and how did they succeed in cheating huge sums of money from honest people. What methods did they use in their "profession" and who are most likely to fall victim to such frauds? I also discuss what finally happened to the great fraudsters and where their spoils disappeared.

One interesting aspect that struck me from the outset is that none of my major money criminals is a woman. It also emerged that the proportion of women who have fallen victim to the frauds is vastly smaller than that for men. Are women really more honest than men? Are they more suspicious, more alert? All this is pondered in detail.

Besides five decades of keen observations of the financial world, my book is also based on my extensive financial home library, the wide collections of various university libraries, financial publications, factual reviews on the web and heaps of financial news articles.

Any inaccuracies in the book may partly be due to the fact that police records and court proceedings concerning major frauds are generally not public, or they are scant or contradictory. The accused criminals present their own "truths" and the victims other "facts". For understandable reasons, the police often do not want to disclose the fraudsters' elaborate techniques. Many victims may also have their own reasons for hiding the truth, for instance, the shady origins of their money, or tax frauds.

Money does not normally disappear somewhere; it merely tends to change pockets. It is my hope that this book will prevent many honest people from falling victim to ruthless money fraudsters. However, I am afraid that this may remain an idle hope when one thinks of how easily so many innocent persons have already fallen prey to silver-tongued, merciless swindlers.

Kari Nars
Helsinki, 15 January 2011

THE TAKEOFF

1

Bernard Madon's Nightmare

"Dammit, dammit, dammit!"

The New York Times' fat headline stared straight out at Bernard L Madon, seated at the breakfast table of his posh Manhattan apartment. He almost choked on the coffee and cold shivers went down his spine.

His namesake, that eternally smiling dirty crook, Bernard Madoff, had nicked billions from thousands of innocent victims!

Madon knew instantly that his life savings were gone. Gone forever! His head almost exploded and the walls felt like they were crumbling. What a shame! And all his friends would laugh behind the back of such a fool!

Perhaps the easiest way out would be to take the potent sleeping pills that Dr MacCallan prescribed only last week and then slash the wrists in a nice warm bath.

How could he have been so incredibly stupid, despite his wife Ellen's nagging that their retirement savings should never be placed into that slick guy's incredulous fund. But even she had relented when he told her about the bank statements his long-time partner, Samuel Goldberg, had flashed before his eyes. They confirmed in black and white the tidy profits he had regularly received from Madoff Securities. The thing really worked!

Samuel had even met the Great Guru personally in the Palm Beach Country Club's pompous bar. He was more than impressed. Everybody considered it a great honour to be accepted to Madoff's exclusive fund, a privilege extended only to a few. He paid a decent 15 per cent in annual profits, come hell or high water.

All the millionaires had seen the fund as a safe investment. And best of all: Madoff did not charge a penny in those expensive management fees that many other fund managers use to fleece their clients.

If it was good for these filthy-rich guys who knew how to make loads of money, it was good for me too, he had thought! At the time, he did not yet know that Samuel was a buddy of Madoff's and pocketed generous bonuses for each new investor he brought in.

But worst of all: he, Bernard L. Madon, had bragged about this modern way of getting rich to his trusted rabbi. This holy man's life savings were now truly dispersed like chaff before the heavenly winds. Never, ever, would he dare to look him in the eye again in the synagogue!

Similar feelings of anger and remorse, perhaps even shame as in our imagined scenario, were certainly found in thousands of affluent American families in late 2008 when Madoff's world-class fraud was disclosed.

Nothing New Under the Sun

Swindlers have cheated gullible people ever since money was invented over 2,500 years ago. Already in ancient Rome the warning *caveat emptor*, or buyer beware, was an adage, as was *nil novi sub sole,* "nothing new under the sun".

Interestingly enough, swindling methods have not changed that much in the last hundred years. The crooks have designed various imaginative investment schemes, but the basic techniques have remained the same. Especially after the invention of the pyramid scheme by Charles Ponzi in the early 1900s. Since then, tempting pyramids of different forms and shapes have been launched all over the world.

Most victims have not heeded the clever warning by Sir John Templeton in the 18th century:

> The four most expensive words in the English language are "this time it's different".

Rich market economies and the Internet provide new openings for money fraudsters. Large numbers of people have plenty of money to invest, huge sums can be transferred abroad because countries have liberalised their previous tight foreign exchange controls, and tax havens facilitate portfolio investments and shelter criminal money. Through the Internet, fraudsters can easily reach thousands of prospective victims and disappear as quickly as they appeared.

One modern phenomenon which has paved the way for fraudsters is that in rich and hectic societies, time has become a scarce resource. Aside from their work many busy people find too little time to pay enough attention to their personal money affairs, either in their everyday life or in their investments. As a result, plenty of money earned through hard work disappears into the pockets of slick criminals. Fortunately for the rest of us, most of them have sooner or later found themselves enjoying the "hospitality" of various governments behind bars.

Swindles also have a societal impact in the sense that they weaken social relations between people and sow distrust and hate against those who have engaged others in these disastrous schemes. They may even affect many countries' economies, if the culprits move their billion-dollar loots into foreign tax havens. Governments forego tax revenues and have to charge honest people more taxes.

Dirty Money Burns in Pockets

In their "profession", swindlers do not generally amass money only out of pure greed, or out of an urge to stabilise their economic situation. Studies of crooks in various countries suggest that they use their prey to do something big, to show off to the world, to enjoy their liberty thoroughly. Often, it's simply an effort to demonstrate how important they are. To do something really exciting.

Money is an integrated part of the swindler's liberty. His low self-esteem is boosted by big banknotes. He wants to make an impression by wasting money on expensive goods or services: fine housing, even castles, expensive cars, luxury hotels, yachts, airplanes, gambling, beautiful women and so forth.

Money burns in the pockets of criminals. It is impossible for them to save money, to buy anything other than expensive articles, to leave anything other than over-generous tips in restaurants and hotels. Their money has to be spent in a flashy, boastful way.

Prostitutes speak about honest money and dirty money. Social security benefits, medical compensation payments or other legitimate income are used for "honest living", such as rent or other domestic expenses. Prostitution earnings, on the other hand, are squandered away rapidly on going out, drugs, alcohol, tobacco or trendy clothes. The dirty money is wasted quickly.

The world of the professional swindler is illustrated by a narcissistic drive in a life lived without safety nets, says Dick Hobbs. First-hand accounts of criminals who see "life as a party" confirm the crucial importance for them of "earning and burning money" – as a way of demonstrating their commitment to an identity defined by conspicuous consumption and funded by crime.

Big money fraudsters are generally smart, seasoned and relatively well-educated professionals compared with most other criminals, such as robbers and burglars. For instance, bank robberies are most often haphazard amateur excursions, performed with minimal planning and base levels of competence. Swindlers, on the other hand, do a great deal of meticulous planning before they launch their satanic schemes.

The rich and top effective market economies generate a great deal of hedonistic consumption, partly as a means of showing off. As countries veered in the direction of economic liberalism, or *laissez-faire*, during the heyday of Reaganism in the 1980s, swindlers could have a ball, with loads of easy money at their feet. Their manipulation of people and markets yielded huge financial gains for them.

WORSHIP OF MONEY

2

Money serves three important functions. Firstly, it measures value; for instance, what is the price of a pound of apples or a TV. Secondly, it is a transaction medium for selling or buying goods and services. And finally, it acts as a store of value for savings and purchasing power.

American writer Gertrude Stein once said that what distinguishes man from animal is money. Time is equivalent to money in educated societies.

We live today in the most money-focused societies in history. Money is king. In Europe, in Asia, everywhere, a great number of people admire the American materialistic society, where high income and boastful consumption are the most important guiding stars.

Money, the Driving Force

Money brings power. People who have plenty of money are admired and often acquire a high status in their society.

Money represents abstract human happiness, said German philosopher Arthur Schopenhauer. In his view, people who are no longer capable of enjoying human happiness devote themselves entirely to money.

Money in the form of purchasing power constitutes so important a motivating force for most people that almost nothing else can be compared with it in the world in which we live, said economist Alfred Marshall.

Capitalism does not really need any other religion than the worship of money because money alone is sufficient to feed peoples' hopes and be the basis for their actions, according to economist Christopher Deutschmann. Those who worship money the most always want more of it faster – even the millionaires.

Typically, when legendary banker J. P. Morgan was once asked when a wealthy man has gained enough money to be completely satisfied, his answer was: "When he has earned the following million."

In many circles within our money-focused societies personal wealth is also regarded as a sign of professional competence, social capability and status. Rich people are respected, but also envied – in Europe, it's people like the newspaper tycoon Rupert Murdoch, the airline mogul Richard Branson, Ikea's owner Ingvar Kamprad, or principal owner of L'Oréal, Liliane Bettencourt. In the United States, it's Microsoft's Bill Gates, the great investor Warren Buffett, the business magnate Donald Trump or New York City Mayor Michael Bloomberg, among many others.

The Lust for Money and the Deadly Sins

In wealthy Western countries most people have conveniently forgotten the early Christian teachings, in which money was well remembered when human vices were listed. Without mincing words, the Bible warns us about the dangers and potentially destructive nature of money.

Jesus evicted the moneychangers, the bankers of those days, from the temple. He also taught that it is "easier for a camel to pass through the eye of a needle than for a rich person to be allowed into the Kingdom of God". The apostle Paul considered that "money is the beginning and the root of all evil".

Of course money is not the root of *all* evil. But money is surely the motive for much that is corrupt and fraudulent in the Western world.

The concept of the Seven Deadly Sins in the teachings of the Catholic Church built around the Bible's Book of Proverbs (6:16–19). The term "deadly sin" derives from the belief that if a person dies with an unrepented grave ("deadly") sin on his or her conscience, it is not possible for him or her to see God, that is, to enter Heaven.

In Dante's *La Divina Commedia*, the seven deadly sins are Wrath,

Greed, Sloth, Pride, Lust, Envy and Gluttony. The deadly sins of the swindlers who steal money from other people are, of course, greed, lust for money and envy of other peoples' money. Perhaps even gluttony.

Of course, these serious sins also cause great pain to unsuspecting victims, who, in many cases, are completely ruined; Bernard Madoff's historical scam being a case in point.

As will be seen in this book, there's a good deal of thought in the words of the poet Richard Armour:

> *That money talks*
> *I'll not deny,*
> *I heard it once.*
> *It said "Goodbye".*

MONEY-SWINDLING METHODS

3

Glib and convincing fraudsters pursue their rackets in many imaginative ways. Their techniques are elaborate, even ingenious, as they appeal to the credulity and inherent greed of their victims.

Some Working Methods of Great Money Fraudsters

- Pyramid schemes, such as Ponzi, WinCapita, Madoff
- Sales of non-existing assets, for instance land rights by General MacGregor, the scrap sale of the Eiffel Tower by Lustig
- Securities frauds, embezzlement and money laundering through tax havens, by Vesco and Cornfeld
- Defrauding employees and other securities frauds by Cornfeld
- Generating huge share-price bubbles through false promises and falsified corporate accounts (South Sea Bubble, Kreuger, Enron)

The Appeal of Pyramid Schemes

The most general and smartly-conceived swindling method nowadays is the pyramid scheme. It demands a great deal of planning to make it credible and attractive, and the set-up of a corporation through which money can be channelled.

Once the pyramid scheme gets off to a good start, eloquent, well-dressed and well-mannered salesmen contact thousands of selected potential clients and promise them tidy profits, from Madoff's 10 to 15 per cent per annum and no management fees, up to hundreds of per cent (Ponzi, WinCapita). Investors are always attracted by imaginative and well-prepared marketing arguments and complicated calculations concerning superprofitable foreign exchange, stock market or other speculative transactions.

The "beauty" of the pyramid technique, from the swindler's perspective, is that from the very beginning it creates a solid impression that "the system really works". The promised profits are dutifully paid in cash or to the bank accounts of early investors – in Ponzi's case, at an annual rate of 360 per cent. The bonus-driven sales agents often even flash bank statements in the face of their clients, confirming that the profits had been paid in full and on time. Through word of mouth, the rumour spreads that such quick profits can easily be made by anyone interested.

The early profits are paid from the next investors' capital input, since these pyramid schemes practically never pursue any of the genuine profit-making business they are allegedly engaged in. Typical examples of this were Ponzi and Madoff.

Another attraction of pyramid schemes is that investors are often so enamoured of their initial high profits that they put in more new capital as well as reinvest their original input and nice profits. This way the liquidity leakage from the pyramid is minimised – and, ultimately, the losses of the investors maximised.

Some of the first investors who have already received promised large profits and therefore believe in the system are hired as especially effective sales agents. They are paid generous fees for each new investor they bring in.

The marketing process benefits from both locally-respected agents, who can create trustful relations with prospective victims, and from others with close personal relations, such as father and son, brothers, other relatives, job colleagues, sporting friends or fellow believers. These special agents are regarded "as one of us". Their testimony is far more convincing than statements by "unreliable" media, dull bank managers or complete strangers.

Rumours about their success spread like wildfire. But eventually, the going gets tougher and tougher when the inward money flow trickles out or the authorities close the fund and the police investigations start.

White-Collar Crime and the Law

Swindles are usually based on fabricated profit promises and/or faked asset values. Together with commercial bribery, stock exchange manipulation, embezzlement and tax frauds, they are part of what the infamous Al Capone once named "the legitimate rackets".

Commenting on the widespread white-collar crime some decades ago in the United States, and comparing it with the political scene, John Flynn stated:

> "The average politician is the merest amateur in the gentle art of graft compared with his brother in the field of business."

Contrary to many other crimes, swindles such as pyramids take place within a predominantly legitimate business environment. Their success is reinforced by the fact that the perpetrators are held as honest people, not as criminals. Take, for instance, Madoff, who was widely admired as a reputable stock market magnate.

Another prominent feature is that these frauds are committed in a private context, with a strong profit motive as a lever. The members of the swindlers' business organisations are protected from detection by the veil of privacy. This privacy is inherent in the relatively complex and specialised work and context of the organisation used. Its activities remain opaque to outsiders, and also to the investors-cum-victims.

The privacy facade provides swindlers with abundant opportunities to denounce any accusations of fraud. The illegitimacy of the operations is often difficult to prove. Typically, a legal contest ensues about the degree to which the purported swindle may be categorised formally as an abuse and, if so, what the appropriate punishment might be, as Michael Clarke stated.

The punishments for these crimes are not always criminal ones, such as jail sentences. On the contrary, many swindlers have escaped criminal sanctions, but received civil sanctions, such as considerable fines.

As business crimes often involve political or juridical processes over the right juridical labels and sanctions, the odds are not stacked in favour of the prosecutors. Crimes such as robbery or burglary are more straightforward from the law's point of view.

Unlike crimes such as assault or street crime, public order is rarely violated by swindlers. In business crime there is normally no violence to persons or property. The transactions are conducted in private rather than in public places, and between people who have a business relationship.

Swindles become possible only if the victims enter into a situation where they can be deceived and defrauded by the offender, whose trustworthiness has been established. These factors account for the far less threatening character of swindles, as there is an absence of any physical damage.

They also partly explain the sometimes limited interest of the police in certain swindles. First, quite understandably, the police see the maintenance of order in the public realm as their primary responsibility. It covers conventional crimes (murders, assaults, burglaries, etc.) which disturb the public order and damage the interests of private citizens.

Second, the police and other public agencies cannot normally gain access to private premises (such as offices and homes) to pursue inquiries unless they have reasonable grounds to suspect that a criminal offence has taken place. These restraints on the power of public authorities also act to protect the swindlers' domains and complicate the official investigations.

Third, the complex nature of the swindles makes them difficult to investigate. The pre-existing relationship between victim and offender easily leads to situations where claims and counterclaims compete.

Finally, the police may take the view that the victims have only themselves to blame for their lack of caution. Or that the victims have the necessary resources to try to recoup at least part of their losses through their own lawyers, or by themselves through civil litigation.

Multilevel Marketing May Remind Us of Pyramids

Schemes reminiscent of pyramids have occurred also in the multilevel marketing sector. One well-known selling organisation was Holiday Magic, founded in 1964. It distributed goods such as home care products and cosmetics.

Holiday Magic's existing distributors were encouraged to recruit additional distributors in an ever-growing multilevel marketing structure, which was later characterised as a pyramid scheme. With the help of the rapidly expanding network, many members actually earned more by marketing sales rights to new members than by selling their products.

Holiday Magic's saga lasted for about ten years. In June 1973 the US Securities and Exchange Commission (SEC) filed a lawsuit against its founder, William Penn Patrick (who had earlier gone through bankruptcy and several business failures), for bilking 80,000 people out of more than $250 million (some $1.2 billion today) through his Holiday Magic soap and cosmetics empire.

The company was also investigated by the Federal Trade Commission and, in June 1973, it was found guilty of deceptive trade practices. A compromise settlement with approximately 31,000 class members establishing a trust fund worth about $2.6 million was approved by the court in May 1974. The organisation was dissolved in 1974, subsequent to the death of Patrick.

Another large company, Amway, is a direct-selling company and manufacturer using multilevel marketing to sell a variety of products. They are primarily items for the health, beauty and home care markets.

The American company was founded in 1959 and is based in Michigan. Its global sales were $8.4 billion in 2009 and it has 13,000 employees. Amway conducts business through a number of affiliated companies in more than 90 countries and territories around the world. *Forbes Magazine* has ranked it one of the largest companies in the United States, and Deloitte deems it one of the largest retailers in the world.

Amway's success has been based on the model that each member in his or her turn seeks to recruit new members into an exponentially growing network. Those who do so receive special benefits. If a member recruits five new members and they, in their turn, also recruit five new members each, he/she will receive income from 25 persons. And if all of these then recruit five new members each, then that first person earns from 125 persons.

Amway has also been accused of being a pyramid. However, in 1979 the US Federal Trade Commission, and in 2008 a court in the United Kingdom, dismissed these claims. They determined that Amway is not a pyramid scheme since its compensation system is based on retail sales to consumers, rather than payments for recruiting.

The Commission, nevertheless, ordered Amway to stop retail price fixing and allocating customers among distributors. It also prohibited Amway from misrepresenting the amount of profit, earnings or sales that its distributors are likely to achieve with the business. It pointed out that half of the distributors do not make any money, and the average distributor, less than $100 a month.

Amway has been marketed as a Christian activity and has close connections with the Pentecostal Movement.

Corporate Fraud Techniques

Large-scale money swindling cannot be pursued without an organisation, sometimes in the form of a bogus company. It is to a high degree a typical corporate crime. The use of a corporation with an appropriate high-flying name (for instance Bernard L. Madoff Investment Securities, WinCapita or Overseas Investors Services) reinforces the credibility of a scheme. It would look suspicious if such vast operations were conducted in the name of a few physical persons and through their personal bank accounts. I classify them as external corporate frauds.

But there are other corporate financial crimes *within* the corporation, what I call internal corporate frauds, which also have a wide scope. In some cases, the perpetrators of pyramid schemes are guilty of two-pronged crimes: defrauding outside victims and using internal methods, such as tax and accounting frauds, concurrently.

The internal type of financial frauds occurs in many different types of corporations, from quite small ones to world-size corporations such as the Enron case to be discussed later. One typical fraud is through diversions by falsifying corporate accounts, financial benchmarks or tax returns.

In its internal corporate frauds, Enron used complicated, "creative" accounting in order to fool investors, stock analysts, authorities and the general public. The most important among these practices was the use of a network of tax haven companies embellishing Enron's accounts.

Such dishonesty was facilitated by globalisation, the loosening of foreign exchange controls and attractive tax havens. Enron's accounts were so complicated and non-transparent that not even seasoned accounting experts, including Arthur Andersen, could detect that the company was running huge losses, instead of its reported profits.

The Center for Financial Research & Analysis (CFRA) has listed seven major financial shenanigans by which fraudulent companies can mislead investors, banks, tax authorities and other interest groups, and create a rosier picture of the companies' economic situation – with potentially serious consequences if, after the truth is discovered, their bank loans default, or their shares collapse.

For instance, in the case of Enron – which at the time was branded the "most important corporate scandal of our lifetime" – its share price dwindled from $90 dollars to less than $1, followed by its bankruptcy.

The main methods identified by CFRA and mentioned in Howard Schilit's book can be summarised as follows:

Seven financial shenanigans used to trick investors and other stakeholders

- Recording Revenue Too Soon or of Questionable Quality (+)
- Recording Bogus Revenue (+)
- Boosting Income with One-Time Gains (+)
- Shifting Current Expenses to a Later or Earlier Period (+ or –)
- Failing to Record or Improperly Reducing Liabilities (+)
- Shifting Current Revenue to a Later Period (–)
- Shifting Future Expenses to the Current Period as a Special Charge (–)

> + = improves the profit figures of the company
>
> – = reduces the profit figures, for instance, in order to create reserves for the future or reduce taxes

These general financial shenanigans are divided into 30 different techniques, through which the tricks are made in practice.

In addition to these techniques, companies may use different off-balance sheet operations which remain outside the normal accounts. Such operations were used by Enron on a large scale. Another rapidly growing type of crime is the use of falsified bills and receipts and even falsified bank statements.

Insider trading has been a typical type of swindle in the corporate and banking world. Ivan Boesky, a prominent broker in New York, amassed in the 1980s a fortune of some $200 million by betting on corporate takeovers on the basis of tips that he received from corporate insiders.

Although insider trading of this kind was illegal, laws prohibiting it were rarely enforced until Boesky was prosecuted by the Securities and Exchange Commission (SEC). Boesky cooperated with the SEC and informed them about other scams, including those of financier Michael Milken.

The prestigious investment bank, Drexel Burnham Lambert, and one of its top executives, Michael Milken, was the big star of the high-yield bond industry, also called junk bonds, during the 1970s and 1980s. In 1989 he pleaded guilty to six securities and reporting violations, but was never convicted of racketeering or insider trading.

Milken was barred from the securities industry and was sentenced to ten years in prison. After the presiding judge reduced his sentence for cooperating with testimony against his former colleagues and for good behaviour, he was released after less than two years.

Milken is nowadays one of America's richest men, with a net worth of $2.1 billion in 2007. He is known as a philanthropist supporting medical research and education.

The classic small-scale corporate swindle is the long firm credit fraud. Initially, the perpetrator's company (a consultancy, shop, restaurant, manufacturing firm or something else) builds up its creditworthiness image for some time by making prompt payments for its purchases. In the following stage, on the strength of its good payments record it takes as much credit as possible from banks and its suppliers of goods and services. Finally, the owner (or owners) disappears with the cash money.

Grey List of Fiscal Paradises

The current "Grey List" of fiscal paradises published by the OECD in 2009 includes the following 20 countries or other jurisdictions – of which only one is European, Andorra:

- Andorra
- Anguilla
- Antigua and Barbuda
- The Bahamas
- Belize
- Montserrat
- Nauru
- Niue
- Panama
- St Kitts and Nevis

- Cook Islands
- Dominica
- Grenada
- Liberia
- Marshall Islands
- St Lucia
- St Vincent and the Grenadines
- Samoa
- Turks and Caicos Islands
- Vanuatu

Part of the money circulating through tax havens originates from speculation by banks and companies, but also from money laundering related to the international drug trade or to swindlers who hide their loot. Cases in point were money laundering by such banks as Banco Ambrosiano, one of Italy's largest banks, which failed in 1984 as a result of speculation, and from the Bank of Credit and Commerce International, which collapsed in 1991.

The global banking crisis from 2007 onward has increased the pressure to enact political initiatives in the United States and the European Union, with a view to tightening the supervision and control of banks and international capital flows. Many tax havens may already have seen their heyday.

But it is obviously impossible to create a completely watertight supervision system. There will always be room for inventive and/or immoral states, banks, enterprises and people willing to help swindlers find loopholes that facilitate their bad deeds.

The Cayman Islands has become the fifth largest banking centre in the world. It hosts about 280 foreign banks, including well-known names such as HSBC, Goldman Sachs and UBS. In addition, as the world's leading off-shore hedge fund jurisdiction, it has over 10,000 such fund registrations. There's no income tax, no capital gains tax or corporation tax, only import duties. The Cayman Islands is not included in OECD's Grey List.

The Equity Funding Corporation Scam

One interesting example of a big corporate swindle was the Los Angeles-based financial conglomerate, Equity Funding Corporation, in the 1960s and early 1970s. The company was established in 1960 and moved into the glittering world of high finance. It flourished in the heady economy called the "go-go" years.

The firm was designed to appeal to its customers' greed from the very beginning, according to Professor James William Coleman. It marketed a package of mutual funds and life insurance to private individuals. They received a loan against their shares as collateral, and that loan was, in its turn, used to pay the insurance premiums.

Initially the idea was that the programme would end after ten years, with the customers making a large cash payment to clear their loans, presumably with the money they had made from the increasing value of their mutual fund shares. Of course, the whole scheme worked only as long as the stock market did not plummet. And because an economic downturn seemed unlikely amid the buoyant optimism of the time, the optimistic investors put their trust in the company.

Equity Funding's insurance and investment business expanded at a phenomenal rate in the 1960s due to reports that it generated enormous profits. In reality the company lost money from the very start. Michael Clarke stated that it reported $85 million of non-existent commission income. It also created a huge number of bogus insurance, at a value of $2 billion, to generate more cash from the sale of these policies onward to reinsurers.

Its directors resorted to one of the most common techniques of business fraud to keep the company afloat: they juggled the books to give the company a false veneer of success. This upped the share price and the willingness of bankers to provide loans to the company.

Five years after the Equity Funding went public, the stock had risen from $6 to an astronomical $80 a share. Five years later, the firm's equity was almost worthless.

Over a hundred Equity executives were aware of the massive accounting fraud, which included a computer system entirely dedicated to creating and maintaining fictitious insurance policies. But they disclosed nothing to the authorities. It is unclear if they were motivated by company loyalty, greed or fear.

The SEC did not detect Equity Funding's racket in time. The evidence suggests that the SEC's intelligence at the time was passive, haphazard and fortuitous. However, the final nail in the coffin was driven by an employee who, disgruntled by his layoff, leaked damning information to a securities analyst.

Ten thousand investors, some of them major institutions, held stocks worth $228 million (some $1.1 billion today) before the company finally came to an end after a run of some 12 years. The subsequent investigation in 1973 showed that Equity had written 56,000 bogus insurance policies, created $120 million in phony assets, and even "killed" some of the phoney insurees in order to collect on their life insurance policies.

The corporation collapsed after the facts came to light. Equity's president, Stanley Goldblum, received an eight-year jail sentence for his offences, and numerous other conspirators had shorter terms. Estimates of the total losses varied, but ran as high as $3 billion today. Investors were paid just 12 cents to the dollar.

Criteria for Successful Conmen

Very few people could succeed as big money fraudsters. It requires many talents: social skills, good manners, a psychological eye and steely nerves. A common criminal, for instance, a robber or thief, would never manage in this demanding "profession".

The fraudster has to gain the trust of those who are targeted as victims through his convincing and gentlemanly behaviour. With the help of sophisticated planning, people are manipulated to fall prey to the swindler.

Victor Lustig, who preferred to introduce himself as a noble Austrian count, may perhaps be called the world champion of fraudsters. He was active in this field in the 1920s and 1930s in the United States and Europe – until he was sent to spend his retirement days in the much feared Alcatraz prison in San Francisco Bay. Lustig listed some simple preconditions for success in his special field.

Lustig's Ten Commandments for Successful Fraudsters

- Dress and behave nicely
- Listen patiently to the victims
- Do not speak rapidly or nervously
- Never look bored
- Wait until the victim reveals any political opinions, then agree with them
- Let the victim express any views on religion, sports, food, patriotism etc., then agree completely
- Never discuss illness, unless some special concern is shown
- Do not pry into personal matters (the victim will usually start to talk about them soon)
- Never boast – just let them understand how important you are
- Never appear intoxicated

Professional swindlers plan their projects carefully: they take their time to prepare them, establish a detailed strategy for the process from the beginning till the end, figure out their prospective "clients" and their preferences, hire capable assistants helpful in creating trustful relations with the victims, etc. They may use months, perhaps even years, in the planning process before launching their operations.

The most important prerequisite for success is, of course, a winning personality, an ability to persuade and talk people round. A sense of humour is also a useful virtue in this demanding racket, as shown by the ten swindlers scrutinised later in this book. In addition these criminals have to be quite egoistic, sly and flexible.

Fraudsters must be able to enjoy the good things in life because that makes it easier to approach their prospective victims. They are often too lazy or impatient to work in a normal, nine-to-six honest job or to lead a normal existence – and that's one of the drivers for their crimes.

Furthermore, financial fraudsters must have organisational skills, particularly for preparing extensive pyramid schemes and maintaining their credibility long enough to collect rich loots. Bernard Madoff was able to pursue his mendacious life and criminal activities successfully for 15 to 20 years, without creating too much overt suspicion.

Finally, the marketing of grand pyramid schemes to thousands of people requires a grasp of money and capital markets and portfolio investments. And an ability to explain the investment plan in a professional, convincing and tempting manner. Small crooks do not at all meet these exacting standards.

What is a Conman?

The American word *conman* comes from *confidence man*, a synonym for swindler. The term was coined by US newspapers in 1849, after the New York court trial of William Thompson.

Thompson fulfilled many of the success criteria discussed above. In the late 1840s he operated in New York City, which at the time was a rapidly-growing urban society marked by anonymity, confusion and rapidly increasing wealth. These conditions encouraged all manners of frauds, forgeries and "confidence" schemes such as the ones pioneered by Thompson. The New York police estimated that during the 1860s one out of ten professional criminals in New York was a confidence man.

The scenario was straightforward: a gentlemanly-dressed Thompson would approach an upper-class perfect stranger, a target (victim of a swindle). He pretended that they knew each other, and began a brief conversation. After gaining the target's trust, Thompson would ask: "Have you confidence in me to trust me with your watch until tomorrow?"

The stranger supposed that Thompson was some old acquaintance whom he or she could not for the moment recollect, and allowed him to take the watch. Upon taking the watch, or occasionally money, Thompson would depart laughing, and the stranger thought it was a joke. But after that, he never saw Thompson again – or the watch.

Thompson was finally caught when one (watch-less) victim recognised him in the street. He turned out to be an "old graduate" of the Sing Sing maximum security prison, located in the village of Ossining (from which the Sing Sing name is derived) on the Hudson River in New York State.

He received a new prison sentence at the 1849 trial. The Thompson case was a major inspiration and source for Herman Melville's novel of 1857 called *The Confidence-Man*.

Money Swindlers: The Nobility of Criminals

Swindlers are members of a criminal elite. They make vastly more money from their crimes than other criminals. They run fewer physical risks. Their chances of arrest or conviction are smaller, and if convicted they often (with the exception of Madoff) receive lighter penalties – partly because they, usually as defendants in civil courts, enjoy the advantages of wealth, prestige, power of speech, convincing manners and the best legal representation.

Those who hunt them down, the police and especially the financial regulatory agencies, are almost always underfunded and understaffed, especially in comparison with the resources of the high-level swindlers which they are supposed to police – a fact that became abundantly clear, for instance, in the Madoff scheme.

Common professional thieves, if and when they speak honestly, admit that they are thieves. White-collar fraudsters basically see themselves as fairly honest men, perhaps breaking a few laws on the fringes, but certainly not as major criminals. In their own mind, some of them may even regard themselves as a kind of "financial Robin Hood", who help at least some of their fellow men to make big money.

Occasionally, some white-collar criminals have even created an aura of glory around themselves in the media, like the confidence trickster and cheque forger Frank Abagnale. His career was the subject of a book, *Catch Me If You Can,* and a Hollywood film.

The dressy term, "white-collar" crime, launched by American sociologist Edwin Sutherland in 1949, has been translated into many languages: in French, *crime en col blanc*, in Italian, *criminalita in colletti bianchi*, in German, *Weisse-Kragen Kriminalität* and in Spanish, *el delito de cuello blanco.*

All financial crimes require three basic preconditions: motivation, opportunity and the breaking of trust. I will discuss the motivational factors later. Without opportunity, there is no crime. High crime rates reflect the presence of attractive criminal opportunities. In great swindles, the perpetrators are breaking the trust of people whom they attract as investors into their fraudulent schemes.

The central principle is the ability to convince gullible potential victims that they can make big money. Defrauding money from people is, to a large degree, a question of acting. Those who cannot internalise this working method will not succeed in this "profession".

Successful fraudsters live by being alert, sharp and witty, in order to gain the confidence of people. They firmly believe in the adage "There's a sucker born every minute".

The Danger of Getting Caught

In designing their intricate schemes, the swindlers of course also assess the probability of getting caught and the related punishment. In most countries, especially in Europe, the sentences for financial crimes have been rather lenient, often only a few years in jail or even suspended jail sentences, fines and fairly low indemnities.

In the United States the sentences are much harsher: from prison sentences of 10 to 20 years, up to Madoff's record-breaking 150 years. Even in Europe the punishments have become more severe in recent years.

If the risk of getting caught does not seem too high (especially since many criminals typically underestimate this negative outcome) compared with the prospective monetary benefits, many fraudsters consider the potential "net gain" worth the risk.

It is similar to the renowned economist Charles P. Kindleberger's "agency problem", the propensity in a world of egotistical materialism for the agent to cheat his principal for his own advantage if he can do that without getting caught – or, if caught, without suffering a penalty greater than his gain.

In the past, American white-collar racketeers were often seen only as shrewd businessmen rather than genuine criminals. It would have been almost un-American to label captains of industry or leading bankers common criminals. Even if their misdeeds cost the American society billions.

Professional swindles may, in some cases, be likened to stealing candy from a baby.

In contrast to the swindlers' strong position and image, their victims are in general weak. They are mostly unorganised, have insufficient information about the details of the fraud, do not have recourse to the best lawyers and lack technical expertise. Consequently, they cannot protect themselves very efficiently.

A burning lust for money is of course a dominant character trait among swindlers. They must have a high risk tolerance as there is always the danger of getting caught. But compared with the prospect of phenomenal earnings, they may regard the risk only as a "job-related risk". I also have the feeling that many swindlers are quite self-assured optimists who suppress the thought of capture.

Since many financial crimes are quite complicated constructions requiring much imagination and planning on the part of the swindlers, police investigations are time-consuming and technically demanding. Individual crimes normally concern only one or a few parties, whereas extensive pyramid schemes involve thousands of victims. Contacting and interrogating them demands tens, if not hundreds, of police agents.

The judiciary process is further complicated by the international aspects of these crimes, such as chains of foreign exchange transfers, fronting companies and money laundering in tax havens.

HOW ARE MILLION-DOLLAR FRAUDS POSSIBLE?

4

"The stupid guy's foods are eaten first."
(Old Russian proverb)

Swindlers exploit all human weaknesses, such as greed, vanity and credulity, in their despicable "profession". They also benefit from peoples' virtues such as honesty, empathy, or wide-eyed belief in the trustworthiness of their fellow beings. Besides, most victims dream about enriching themselves rapidly. This vision spurs them forward towards the abyss.

Professional fraudsters instinctively recognise if a potential victim is either gullible or a fool. That greatly helps the "marketing effort". But of course not all targets are greedy, wide-eyed, stupid, dishonest or uneducated.

The swindlers may also exploit their victims' possible dishonesty. Investors looking for sky-high profits are often seeking even higher net gains through tax evasion, breaking accounting rules or evading foreign exchange regulations. There are reasons to suspect that at least part, if not a great deal, of the profits of pyramid investors, remain unreported in tax returns or hidden in foreign bank accounts.

If a pyramid investor resorts to tax or other manipulations, that may create a closer relationship with the swindler. Or the fear that his or her deceit may be leaked to the authorities may also lead to this.

Criminals have a saying that it is difficult or almost impossible to cheat exceedingly honest persons. Swindlers tend to avoid such individuals.

They are helped by the fact that most people have an innermost urge to believe in something, sometimes even in lies: for instance, in sales agents proposing ultra-attractive pyramid investments in a smooth and convincing way. Besides, in the course of their lives, most people sometimes do something foolish, which also paves the way for crooks. Opportunity makes the thief.

All financial dealings are based on trust, otherwise they would not be made. Trust is an essential underlying requirement. For instance: clients of banks or investment funds put their trust in the competence and honesty of the organisation, believing that an investment scheme presented to them will operate on the stated terms and will be managed honestly. Investors in pyramid schemes of course also trust that they will get their generous profits and their stakes back, otherwise they would not put their money at risk.

Smart and nimble fraudsters are frequently one step ahead of financial supervision authorities and their "clients", which explains why they are able to conceal their criminal activities at least for some time.

A famous quote attributed to Abraham Lincoln says that "You can fool some of the people all of the time, and all of the people some of the time, but you cannot fool all of the people all of the time." For crooks such as pyramid operators, the first part of this quote suffices. They need only to succeed in fooling just a minute fraction of all people.

The Heap of Lies

Lying and self-deception are deeply embedded in human life and interaction. Everybody lies, at least sometimes, even if they are mainly small white lies.

Swindles are of course also based on lies. People's gullibility offers an excellent working platform for swindlers. Most of their victims really want to believe that they can earn big money, that they themselves are smarter than the average person and that they really deserve to be successful.

As a matter of fact, a large part of the public is ready to collude with or connive at some illegal or underhand practices, as intimated by a simple question posed by the British researcher Michael Clarke: How many people voluntarily insist on paying value added tax, VAT, when they have their plumbing fixed, their windows repaired or their car serviced?

Recent British research concludes that the best estimate of the size of the black economy is about three to five per cent of GDP, which adds up to quite a few billion. It points to widespread collusion of impropriety and misappropriation in many countries.

In its strong form, these activities may represent cheating, tax evasion or even worse. But the people involved in these activities do not generally regard themselves as criminals, even though they perhaps recognise that they break the law. A respected businessman or artisan who evades taxes usually considers himself perhaps a petty offender, but surely not a criminal.

An example from the banking world: one of the branch offices of the Bank of Helsinki was the scene of a break-in some decades ago. The burglars drilled a hole into the large cellar vault from the next-door cellar the night before a long holiday weekend. They had all the time in the world to pry open a large number of the bank's clients' custody lockers.

According to the normal practice for custody safekeeping, the bank did not have exact information about the custody contents. When it requested information about its clients' losses afterwards, surprisingly many claimed that they had stored a fair deal of gold, jewellery or cash in their safes. The bank was forced to indemnify its clients on the basis of many more or less exaggerated claims.

Even in non-criminal contexts – for instance, when a bank's portfolio investment adviser (whose more appropriate title, by the way, might be sales manager) paints a rosy picture of some equity funds or shares – the underlying risks connected with the investment are often understated or suppressed. Generally the investment advisers do not of course tell outright lies to the client, but the full facts are not necessarily presented in a completely balanced way, because they want to succeed in making a sale.

Many scam victims have a high risk tolerance. For instance, in the WinCapita pyramid scheme, a number of investors had a background of money games and sports betting. They were not interested in the meagre one or two per cent interest on bank deposits, but dreamt about big and fast profits. They represented the type of investors who had a high opinion of their own intelligence.

Surprisingly enough, only few pyramid investors seem to bother to familiarise themselves in detail with the swindlers' complex investment constellations, which are supposed to generate the alleged copious profits. On the other hand, most people would never understand them anyway, as they are either incomprehensible (WinCapita), not open to analysis as a "business secret" (Madoff), or outright bluffs.

They *wanted* to believe in the scheme, in the lie, since Madoff had a solid reputation as an accomplished and widely-respected investment guru.

The marketing of utopian moneymaking schemes is much facilitated by the fact that hardly anybody poses the right critical questions. The old Finnish saying that "stupidity is condensed in masses", that investors move in herds, is not taken from the wind.

Occasionally some investors have tried to fool swindlers – usually with the result that they soon realise they have been manipulated all along, although initially they imagined having drawn a winning number.

Investments Based on Trust

When people invest money, personal experiences have the greatest bearing. But they also trust the advice of people who are close to them, for instance, relatives, friends, colleagues.

The trust we place in others also depends on their and our own social and economic environment. The more similar they are, the more the confidence. People who put billions of dollars into Bernard Madoff's fund entrusted their money to him partly because he was like them – or at least as they would want to be – friendly, respected, successful, rich and a stylish member of social circles. Many investors also had the same Jewish background as Madoff.

But people invested with Madoff also because many of them were busy millionaires, with a hectic lifestyle. Since their time was so scarce and valuable, a closer scrutiny of Madoff's investment fund – how his stable 10 to 15 per cent annual profits were possible year in, year out, never mind whether stock markets were up or down – would have been quite costly in terms of their expensive time. It could perhaps even have caused embarrassment to their "great friend".

Thus some of the millionaires familiar with large business deals and usually making loads of money were perhaps even more credulous than other victims.

Relationship Between Swindler and Victim

Money swindling is based on a dynamic relationship between the fraudster and the victim, the target. A professional swindler easily senses his victim's weaknesses and exploits them fully – be it avarice in the extreme, gambling fever or financial setbacks which the investor tries to overcome with the promised fabulous profits.

The trap is designed patiently in order to make it look credible and trustworthy. Part of the swindler's tactic is to start by giving some unimportant or irrelevant information. The target knows this information himself or imagines that it is completely true, which makes him feel comfortable. The rest of the information is aimed at making the whole story even more convincing.

One example: sales agents marketing pyramid investments frequently slander the banks for paying pitifully low deposit interest rates, or for bad investment advice or bureaucracy. This makes their own fast way to riches look much better – while the "greedy banks are conning people".

The deception succeeds since most people do not overtly want to question other peoples' honesty. The fraudster also anticipates the victims' doubts and learns how to disarm them by first addressing these doubts himself, calming down the target.

Some psychiatrists consider that swindlers and victims are bound together in a symbiotic love-hate relationship from which both take satisfaction and depend on, according to Kindleberger. It is akin to the "Stockholm syndrome", a psychological state in which hostages may develop a sympathetic attitude towards their hijackers.

The fraudster seeks to establish good personal contact with the victim by talking about some joint event from the past, or a common friend, an acquaintance or relative, shared political or religious beliefs or making a comment which flatters local patriotism. He may also take up some common hobbies such as golf, fishing or tennis.

Any joint links of this type are useful in dispelling the victim's natural apprehensions. Using these methods, the swindler gains a place in his life and takes something away. Most people feel that they can surely trust nice, well-behaved people with whom they can get along so well.

Because the profits distributed in the initial stages of pyramid schemes consolidate the trust relationship with investors, they normally plough their first profits back into the fund in the hope of reaping even heftier gains. Such reinvestments were quite common in the Ponzi, WinCapita and Madoff cases, after the victims had first enjoyed real big "paper" profits. This credulity and greed accelerated their losses when the bubble finally burst.

The market place and its modes of operation provide the dominant dynamism in Western economies. Therefore, it is no surprise that swindlers have inherited many of its legitimate operational techniques in their profession. They actually adopt eye-catching entrepreneurial strategies, as pointed out in the *Oxford Handbook of Criminology*.

In this vein, pyramid schemes use many elements familiar from normal investment projects: presentation of the project, plenty of background information and strong sales arguments, extensive marketing to people who may be interested in investing in such a speculative scheme, presentation of detailed profit calculations (albeit false), profit payment plan, etc. Key technological inventions in the field of communications have created an environment in which criminals can provide such information easily within countries and even globally to thousands of people.

Since the loss of lifelong savings earned through years of dedicated work is obviously a horrifying experience for anybody, it is not uncommon that in their desperation some fraud victims commit suicide. This happened both in the context of Madoff's fund, General MacGregor's fraud in England, and WinCapita's pyramid in Finland.

What happens to the other victims? The obvious recourse of swindled victims is to turn to the police. The police may, however, be recalcitrant to act and usually do so only if there is clear evidence of a criminal offence or the number of complaints becomes large.

In any case, the victims are caught in a dilemma. As Michael Clarke states in *Business Crime*, the law is slow, uncertain and expensive. Worse still, at the end of the day, legal action will probably have the effect of closing down the swindling organisation, leaving little behind. It may of course be in the public interest to prevent even more people being ensnared as new victims, but the closure of the pyramid may work against the interests of existing victims who would like to try to recoup at least part of their money.

The victims' recourse to the law and public agencies, including the police, is in fact often indicative of understandable despair and a thirst for vengeance. However, some victims may prefer to keep matters in the private realm and attempt to negotiate a civil solution. It may even be in the interest of the swindlers (and perhaps also the victims) to continue negotiations for as long as possible by making offers, promises and part payments.

Do Swindlers Repent Their Bad Deeds?

If a normal person does something unlawful, he or she reacts by feeling shame or regret. An undecided distress creeps in, a fear of what other people may think and what the possible penalties might be.

The inner thoughts of criminals do not follow this pattern. Studies concerning the attitudes of prisoners show that they feel it is vitally important to distance themselves from any feeling of guilt and responsibility. Without repressing their guilt, life would become unbearable, as prison researcher Monika Mattson states in her book.

At least on the surface, the question of culpability does not really interest neurotic prisoners. It is well known that prisoners don't even want to talk about the issue of guilt, or feelings related to it. Some years ago I learnt that a top-class Dutch criminal lawyer, who defended incarcerated major drug smuggling suspects in the Mediterranean area, never ever even dreamt of asking his clients if they were guilty, as he regarded such a question "immoral". His working assumption, and surely that of his clients, was always that they were completely innocent.

A lifer wrote to Mattson that 99 per cent of the first-timers in prison saw themselves as innocent. A normal reaction among prisoners is to shift their relation to the crime towards a relation to the verdict. Instead of admitting that "I stole", a burglar would normally say "*they* sentenced me for burglary".

The real culprit was apparently somebody or something else: a difficult childhood, a bad employer, a nasty wife or other relatives, bad company, alcohol or drugs, the "system", a heavy-handed judge, a lack of money, the immoral society or the bad police or other authorities.

At most, the prisoners would admit that "they were just created like this" or ask "what can a man do about his nature". Or they complained about having been subjected to "unjust pressures", and so for that reason, they were innocent.

In the same spirit, criminals typically belittle their victims and, in particular, their sufferings. For this reason I do not for one second believe that those who have defrauded people of money genuinely regret that they have impoverished or even ruined other people. Probably they rather think that the credulous victims who let themselves be cheated just got what they deserved, or that the swindlers themselves needed their money badly.

Many prisoners are actually reported to brag about their frauds along the lines of "stupidity costs" and "those who fell into the trap so easily deserved to be cleaned". Perhaps they also seek to rationalise events by emphasising that the victims didn't really suffer "because they were rich anyway". Probably the main thing the culprits regret is that they allowed themselves to be caught and jailed.

Prisoners often stress how unavoidable everything was, according to Mattson. They sense the immorality and ruthlessness prevailing in our societies: "The world is bad and people are bad", and therefore they feel justified in feeling angry about it. In this way they swing everything in their own favour, backing their own recklessness.

Many crooks actually consider that their own criminal behaviour is in no way divergent compared with the environment and the subculture in which they already belonged in their youth. It only represents acquired learning from their own criminal circles, in the same way as any other types of learning. In their minds, their criminal deeds are deviant only in the eyes of the majority of the (honest) population.

Criminals usually do not think in terms of cause and effect. They are unwilling to take responsibility for their actions and the consequences, and close their eyes even to the most obvious ones. The after-effects of the swindles are the problem of others – for the offender they do not exist.

If imprisoned criminals really regretted their bad deeds, prison suicides would be much more common, as a kind of final atonement. Suicide would be a form of exit. But at least in Finnish prisons – and supposedly also in most other countries – suicides are fairly rare, even if the general rate of suicides in Finland is high by international standards.

In prison, numerous wrist slashings, or "vents", generally represent an illusory suicide attempt, according to Mattson. Their purpose is rather to signal that the prisoner would like to change an existing situation. Occasionally, they may also be aimed at creating trouble for the prison staff.

A few prisoners even make a habit of this type of so-called suicide attempts. However, the overwhelming majority of real suicides among criminals takes place outside prison.

THE MAKING OF MILLION-DOLLAR CRIMINALS

5

Who is a criminal?

The simplest definition of a criminal is: a person who breaks the laws of society. Money swindlers of course belong to this group.

This definition is, however, too wide because it classifies many persons as criminals who would normally not be regarded as such. A fair deal of people occasionally break the law: for instance, speeding, parking illegally, jaywalking, drinking too many beers before driving, hiding some income in tax returns, denting another car in a parking lot, or taking some items from their workplace without permission.

Alternatively, one could classify only those sentenced by the courts for some crime as criminals. That would substantially underestimate the number of criminals since it would ignore the burglars, robbers, swindlers and other criminals who have not been caught.

Currently, a general definition used in criminal psychology is that criminal behaviour signifies *a person who breaks the laws of society in a deliberate, perhaps continuous, way.* The main focus is on *deviant or asocial behaviour.*

A fairly common opinion is that there's an inverse relationship between socio-economic position and crime: the poorer a person is or the lower his or her socio-economic position is, the likelier he or she is to become a criminal. Criminal tendencies may also be related to difficulties in moving forward in society, inherited criminal values or bad company.

The view that criminality is closely associated with poverty is surely not applicable to swindlers. None of those analysed in this book had been poor or brought up in slums or shattered families, and they were seldom problem children or juvenile delinquents, unlike the crooks dealt with in traditional criminology.

Swindling is probably often, just like other systematic criminality, learnt from direct or indirect association with people who have practised such things before, as stated by Geis and Meier. Those who become white-collar criminals generally experienced particular business situations where criminality was a folkway. Gradually they were inducted to such a system of behaviour, just like for any other custom.

Lower-class criminals such as, burglars or robbers, typically start their "careers" in broken homes. They find delinquents and professional criminals in their surroundings who teach them criminal attitudes and crime techniques. But at least in the United States, the inventive geniuses for many swindles tend to be unscrupulous lawyers or business specialists.

Criminal Backgrounds and White-Collar Crimes

Most of the fraudsters discussed in this book came from middle or upper-class families and had a fairly good education. For instance, the Scottish Gregor MacGregor was a general. The great swindler, Victor Lustig, was a mayor's son and went to private schools. The Swedish match king, Ivar Kreuger, came from an affluent family and graduated as an engineer with honours from the country's most prestigious technological university.

Bernard Cornfeld had a university degree in psychology from Brooklyn College and another one in social sciences from Columbia University. Enron's infamous CEO Kenneth Lay was a doctor in economics from Houston University. Bernard Madoff graduated from Hofstra University. And the main suspect of WinCapita, Hannu Kailajärvi, completed an information technology exam at a technical institute.

We have to seek reasons other than a poor childhood, low education and low socio-economic status to explain why these persons have become swindlers. Possibly social jealousy and an overwhelming ambition to rise high up in society played an important role, for instance, for Enron's Kenneth Lay and Madoff.

In addition, certain uninhibited needs and values, such as a great lust for money and the urge to show off and live luxuriously, may also have steered some individuals onto their criminal paths.

Many sociologists agree that criminal behaviour is usually learnt from friends, from colleagues, from reading. Most of our own attitudes, values and definitions are learnt from other people. But there's also some evidence that criminal tendencies may be inherited. Currently it is unknown exactly how genes influence criminal behaviour, but genetics and environment may interact in complex ways. Some criminal behaviour even appears to have a neurological component.

The men who get involved in violent crimes are mostly young, typically 18 years old or a bit older. Their levels of testosterone reach the highest level at around that age. On the other hand, swindlers are practically always older than that because youngsters would hardly be able to succeed in this demanding "profession".

Personality of Swindlers

Personality disorders and thinking errors encourage persons to embark on deviant, criminal behaviour, according to professors David Putwain and Aidan Sammons. The most important of those thinking errors are illustrated in the table. They cover personality disorders and psychological defence mechanisms, such as feelings of worthlessness, need for power and control, lying and fantasies regarding anti-social behaviour. These result in a lack of concern for others and actions that may cause damage to society, for instance, drug misuse, prostitution, hate incidents and abuse involving sexual orientation.

Thinking Errors of Criminal Personalities

Character traits	Automatic errors of thinking	Errors associated with criminal acts
Feelings of worthlessness	Poor decision making	Fantasies of anti-social behaviour
Need for power and control	Lack of trust	Super-optimism
Perfectionism	Failure to assume obligations	
Lying		

Source: According to Yochelson and Samenow, cited in Putwain and Sammons.

Many criminals seem to be super-optimists. They scoff at the dangers related to their crimes and imagine being able to get away with the help of their perceived quick mind and ingenuity. Criminals also show a lower degree of moral reasoning than law-abiding citizens since crime represents a choice of immoral actions.

The outward appearance of fraudsters does not only seem normal, but superlative, says Stanton E. Samenow in his book, *Inside the Criminal Mind.* They commit their crimes not because they need the money or hate humanity or had a terrible childhood. What connects different swindlers is that their self-esteem rises and falls at the expense of others. Their personality traits may even be shared by serial killers.

> *"From very early, the oxygen of the criminal's life is to seek excitement by doing the forbidden,"* according to Samenow.

Why do they do it when they have so much to lose? Many swindlers appear to have a Jekyll and Hyde personality, wavering between respectability and crime. Most of them would probably have done well in an honest job, like Madoff, who had an eminently successful stockbroker career behind him. The simple answer may just be: they want to make huge profits, a big sting, something extraordinary, to show off to the world, to enjoy feeling superior.

The English philosopher, John Locke, published his great opus, *An Essay Concerning Human Understanding*, in 1690. He regarded "uneasiness" as the driving force behind all human endeavours. It is not what people have that spurs them forward, but what they are missing. This creates a feeling of discontent, an everlasting pursuit of satisfaction, for instance through money and riches. In my opinion, Locke's thoughts may also explain the ulterior motives of swindlers: to constantly strive upward, upward, upward, like Madoff.

In planning their schemes as rationally as possible, many swindlers resort to *copycat crimes*. In fact, several of the offenders in this book had evidently heard or read about some similar previous scams. Charles Ponzi probably got the idea about his famous pyramid scheme from the simple pyramid engineered in 1898 by a small New York accountant by the name of William Miller, mentioned in chapter 10. My feeling is that Ponzi's pyramid may also have served as an example, for instance, for the Finnish WinCapita pyramid, and even for Madoff.

The swindlers of course constantly fear exposure and the long legal process, social censure and punishment that might follow. Nevertheless, they decide to steal. Once they have chosen this road, they continue until they are caught or able to flee, like the really rotten rascal, Robert Vesco.

Some psychologists believe that criminal behaviour may be the result of rational choice: that the decision to commit a crime may instinctively be based on a consideration of whether the material gains outweigh the time and money spent on planning and staging, the risk of getting caught, the loss of reputation and the severity of any punishment.

But the criminals' decision-making process cannot, of course, be completely rational as it is constrained by partly unknown factors, including the time available, the reactions of the police, other authorities, the media or the victims, or even good or bad luck.

To sum up: first, the swindler must have economic reasons for launching his operation. Second, he must trust that he has both the opportunity and the necessary know-how and ability to perpetrate the crime. Third, in the words of Dr. Donald R. Cressey in Jaspan's book, *The Thief in the White Collar*, he must overcome the final hurdle, his conscience.

This he may do by rationalising, by telling himself, for instance, that he won't get caught, that he is "only borrowing the money and will return it" or that "the country, the rich people, all the investors, owe it to me".

But the main question still remains: what forces a man whose entire upbringing has emphasised respect for the law and who has managed so well professionally, to violate those laws and risk the shame, if and when the violation is exposed (like Kreuger and Madoff)? That still remains a mystery.

Swindlers Often Sociopaths

Money swindlers typically seem to be sociopaths or, according to older terminology, non-violent psychopaths. A sociopath suffers from antisocial behavioural disorders. According to the American Psychiatric Association, such disorders involve

> "a pervasive pattern of disregard for, and violation of,
> the rights of others that begins in childhood or early
> adolescence and continues into adulthood".

In the United States, an estimated three per cent of men and one per cent of women are classified as sociopaths. Among the prison population, the figure is much higher, perhaps even 30 per cent or more for men.

Main Features of Sociopaths

- Superficial charm and intelligence
- Strong self-esteem, egocentricity and egoism
- Secretiveness and paranoia
- Pathologic lying and dishonesty
- Recurring difficulties with the law, after conning others for personal gain or pleasure
- Lack of empathy
- Lack of remorse or feeling of guilt
- Anti-social behaviour
- Superficial feelings
- Parasitic lifestyle
- Feelings of being victims themselves, hence they feel free to use others for their own purposes
- Failure to assume responsibility for own actions
- Recklessness

The two particularly prominent features of many swindlers, egocentricity and recklessness, were confirmed in a study of 30 British white-collar criminals in the Leyhill Prison, as described in the book, *Criminology in Transition*. Other outstanding features in these offenders' personalities were

> "their ambition, their drive, their desire to mix with people of higher social position than their own, to give their children an expensive private education, and their willingness to take financial risks in the process".

Some criminals are scared of sociopaths cum psychopaths, as expressed in Quentin Tarrantino's film, *Reservoir Dogs*:

> "What you're supposed to do is act like a fuckin'
> professional. A psychopath is not a professional. You
> can't work with a psychopath, 'cause ya don't know
> what those sick assholes are gonna do next."

Despite their superficial charm many sociopaths have difficulties keeping friends, maintaining relationships such as marriage, or dealing with authority figures, such as financial regulators, tax officials or persons within the judicial system.

While fraudsters violate the law because they believe it will bring them more pleasure and less pain than the other courses of action available to them, some of them may also be driven by fear, for instance that they, like Madoff, may lose what they already have.

Women Less Frequently Swindlers and Victims

Historically, in world literature and among the public, women have been either idolised or defamed. According to Joy Pollock in Lee H. Bowker's book:

> "The images of women have fluctuated from paragons
> of virtue to devious enchantresses."

For a long time, female criminality was not considered worthy of the researchers' attention. One of the first works on the topic was Italian professor Cesare Lombroso's and his colleague Guglielmo Ferrero's book, *The Female Offender* in 1894. Before that Lombroso had published his first major work, *The Criminal Man*, in Italian in 1876.

The eccentric Lombroso's basic theory was that the criminal man was a biological throwback to a primitive breed of man. Therefore, criminal types could be recognised by various atavistic degenerate body characteristics, such as low foreheads, excessive facial hair and strong jawbones.

As Lombroso's interest turned to the female criminal, the thesis that criminals were biologically predisposed and recognisable by physical stigmata was true also for female offenders. Criminal women were found to possess many male characteristics, both physical and mental. This masculinity suppressed their maternal drives and induced even more crimes.

According to Lombroso's and Ferrero's peculiar thinking, all women were like big children, with no moral sense and no maturity. Law-abiding women were only amoral children held in check by their piety and sobriety!

Women were also organically conservative and passive, according to Lombroso. This and their feminine qualities, besides piety, maternal instincts and weakness, served to repress criminal tendencies. Physical and psychological factors also worked in the same direction.

Lombroso's theories on criminals have been severely criticised. He seemed to be unaware of basic statistical methods when he made his prison interviews, his sample sizes were far too small and his findings were not statistically significant.

However, Lombroso and Ferrero underlined that women commit far fewer crimes than men. In state and federal prisons in the United States and in most Western European countries, the percentage of women prisoners is minimal: typically only four to seven per cent.

However, if one measures the overall female share of *recorded crime*, it is much higher than the percentage of women prisoners: in the 1980s and 1990s, it was some 16 to 20 per cent in Britain, France and Germany, or three to five times more than the percentage of women prisoners.

Prison statistics tend to underestimate female crime. First of all, policemen are often not that keen to apprehend women, as they may want to appear as "knights in shining armour", according to *The Oxford Handbook*.

Secondly, there seems to be some judicial reluctance to sentence women so harshly that they would go to prison.

Within the judicial systems, women are regarded as in need of protection, not punishment, and are often accorded the respect of chivalry. Criminology textbooks routinely state that women are less likely to be held in custody at the pre-trial stage, less likely to be convicted if tried and, if convicted, more likely than men to avoid imprisonment.

Therefore, it appears that a substantially higher proportion of women than men receives suspended jail sentences, partly as a result of the perhaps even paternalistic attitude of many judges. On the other hand, if the crime has been highly unfeminine (for example, violent manslaughter), the courts respond harshly.

In recent years, women offenders in many countries have actually changed their crime patterns towards the more "masculine" styles. They have become more aggressive and violent.

But normally women tend to commit less serious offences than men. For instance, female shoplifters generally steal fewer items and less expensive products than their male "colleagues". In major frauds or other big crimes, they are mostly not the sole perpetrators, but rather partners, accessories or conspirators who play a secondary role.

Women rarely perform robberies or even burglaries on their own. They are seldom members of organised crime syndicates. As regards the most severe punishment in the United States – the death sentence – 1,189 men have been executed after 1976, compared with only 11 women, less than one per cent. The last time a woman was executed in the United States was on 24 September 2010 when Teresa Lewis was put to death – after an interim period of five years without any female executions.

My personal analysis of woman criminality is summed up on the following page:

Why Are Women Less Criminally Inclined Than Men?

- The most important female identity success factors, such as home, love, children, family, friends and good health cannot be satisfied through crimes.
- Women do not worship money quite as ardently as men.
- Criminological theory underlines the pressures on individuals to succeed in society by any means. These pressures may be less dominant in female identity. High earning ambitions and the need to show off attract fewer women than men into crimes.
- Socially more active women may have a stronger "shame on you" reflex than men: what would possible children, relatives, friends and other people think of them if they got caught?
- Women's biologically inherent greater caution means that they are less likely to generate the aggressiveness and risk-taking that are essential drivers for crime – while the higher testosterone levels of men tend to encourage such courses of action.
- Women tend to be more down-to-earth, realistic and do not fall into the over-optimism trap typical of many male criminals when assessing the possibilities for success or the risks of getting caught.
- The percentage of sociopaths inclined to commit crimes is much smaller among women than men.

An overwhelming 98 per cent of those charged with anti-trust and securities frauds and other SEC violations in the mid-1980s were men. However, while only about 20 per cent of the persons arrested in the United States were female, women have, according to Coleman, made up 35 to 40 per cent of those arrested for embezzlement, and over 40 per cent of those arrested for other types of fraud. The percentage of women arrested for shoplifting is also quite high.

When it comes to women as swindle victims, their behaviour seems to be more cautious than men. For instance, in Finland's suspected WinCapita pyramid, it was estimated that only some 20 per cent of the victims were women. I also have the impression that the proportion of "Madoffed" women was much lower than that for men.

One explanation may be that in most homes, men are typically the main breadwinners and occupy themselves with the family's investments whenever larger decisions are required.

Secondly, women are clearly more cautious than men – women don't walk on roofs – and are perhaps less gullible when fabulous profits are touted to them.

Thirdly, such investments by men may well be part of the male need to show off, or a manifestation of jealousy if they learn that others have made huge profits.

The lower percentage of female victims may also be due to the fact that fewer pyramid salesmen make contact with women as they may suspect that women would pose more critical questions or invest less than men, who are often quick and impulsive decision makers. The agents may also have the fear that talkative women might voice their suspicions widely in their surroundings, thereby hampering the marketing effort.

SPECTRUM OF THE WORLD'S GREATEST FINANCIAL FRAUDS

Historical Swindles and Bubbles

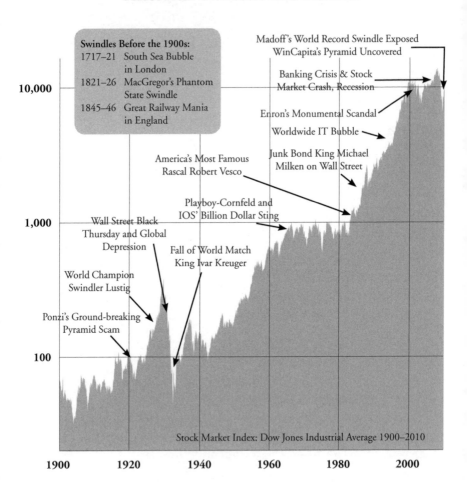

Swindles Before the 1900s:
1717–21 South Sea Bubble
         in London
1821–26 MacGregor's Phantom
         State Swindle
1845–46 Great Railway Mania
         in England

Madoff's World Record Swindle Exposed
WinCapita's Pyramid Uncovered

Banking Crisis & Stock
Market Crash, Recession

Enron's Monumental Scandal

Worldwide IT Bubble

Junk Bond King Michael
Milken on Wall Street

America's Most Famous
Rascal Robert Vesco

Playboy-Cornfeld and
IOS' Billion Dollar Sting

Wall Street Black
Thursday and Global
Depression

Fall of World Match
King Ivar Kreuger

World Champion
Swindler Lustig

Ponzi's Ground-breaking
Pyramid Scam

Stock Market Index: Dow Jones Industrial Average 1900–2010

10,000

1,000

100

1900   1920   1940   1960   1980   2000

The long history of money frauds offers almost unbelievable stories, especially in Great Britain and the United States. Long before the monumental scam of Bernard Madoff, two Britons, Sir John Blunt of the South Sea Company and General Gregor MacGregor, engineered sophisticated financial frauds. Another notable financial criminal was Charles Ponzi, the inventor of the pyramid scheme.

The Czech Victor Lustig may be classified as the world champion of "creative" money frauds. He even succeeded in selling the Eiffel Tower to a gullible Parisian scrap merchant. Later, he defrauded hundreds of people and started extensive currency forgery in the United States – which finally handed him a 20-year prison sentence in Alcatraz.

Global match king Ivar Kreuger was the most celebrated and, in the end, most despised Swedish industrialist. As his worldwide empire crumbled, he committed suicide in his luxurious Paris apartment. The illustrious Bernard Cornfeld with his brilliant Fund-of-Funds invention was the "*enfant terrible*" of the financial world.

"The Undisputed King of Fugitive Financiers" Robert Vesco, and the gigantic Enron's infamous chief executive, Kenneth Lay, cheated billions from thousands of people. In Finland, the WinCapita pyramid scheme is under investigation for defrauding thousands of people of millions of euros.

The Top 10 Historical Swindles
- The South Sea Scheme in London, 1717–1721
- General MacGregor's phantom-nation swindle in England and France, 1821–1826
- The "World Champion Swindler" Victor Lustig's frauds in the 1920s and 1930s
- Charles Ponzi's groundbreaking pyramid swindle in the US in 1920

- The rise and fall of Swedish match king Ivar Kreuger, 1912–1932
- Playboy Cornfeld's sting through International Overseas Services in the 1960s
- The frauds of "America's Most Famous Rascal", Robert Vesco, from the late 1960s onward
- Enron's billion-dollar swindle, 1990–2001
- WinCapita's suspected pyramid scheme in Finland, 2005–2008
- The financial criminal of the 21st century, Bernard Madoff, 1995–2008

Several of the world's great swindlers have met their destiny in the wake of sudden plunges in the business cycles, as illustrated in the diagram at the beginning of this chapter. No wonder economist John Kenneth Galbraith ironically wrote that "Recessions catch what the auditors miss"!

For instance, Ivar Kreuger fell after Black Thursday in 1929 and the Great Depression caused his monumental financing distress in 1929–1932. Bernard Cornfeld's investment fund hit on bad times in 1969–1970 with the shaky stock markets. And Bernard Madoff's fraud of almost biblical proportions came to light in 2008, following the outbreak of the banking and stock market crisis.

Although two of the top 10 swindles took place some 200 to 300 years ago, they could just as well have happened yesterday – so similar are the human psychological foundations for these swindles. This is in line with the old French proverb, "the more things change, the more they remain the same" – *plus ça change, plus c'est la même chose*.

Human lust for money has remained unabated over the last two thousand years, and people's psychological reactions in money matters follow the old patterns. Neither have the basic rules of the game in financial markets changed very much. Speculators speculate, swindlers swindle, and risk-averse individuals invest cautiously.

According to Kindleberger in *Manias, Panics and Crashes,* many speculative booms – and subsequent swindles – commence with sudden economic stimulus and overheating business cycles, as was the case after the great geographical discoveries in the 16th century, the Industrial Revolution in Great Britain and the United States, the stock market craze preceding the economic crisis in the United States in 1929–1930, the IT boom in the 1990s, or the explosive economic growth before the economic and banking crisis in 2007–2009.

The history of manias and panics is replete with examples of destabilising "cobweb" responses to exogenous shocks. At the beginning, there are strong positive signals to banks, companies and investors, followed by spectacular surges in stock prices which attract old and new investors to the security markets. Enchanted by their sense of well-being, equity and housing investors lose grip of their sound judgement.

The objects of speculation vary widely from one mania to the next, from domestic and foreign securities of various kinds, to foreign exchange, derivatives, energy, land, houses, gold, etc. Companies benefit from the euphoria through large share issues. Many investors multiply their profits by leveraging their investments through derivatives or stock loans.

At the top of the business cycle the speculation becomes increasingly ambiguous and spreads out to different types of investments. Towards the end, the speculation tends to detach itself from really valuable objects and turn to delusive ones.

People seek to earn riches without a real understanding of the processes involved (for instance, in banking, the IT sector or in more or less complicated derivatives). That also provides lucrative hunting ground for swindlers promising fabulous speculative profits. They enter the scene to exploit the accelerating greed.

It all erupts due to what Adam Smith in the 1700s described as "folly, negligence… knavery and extravagance".

However, at some point, the first investors begin to sell and cash in their profits. Finally, the specific signal that starts the general collapse may be the failure of a bank or a big firm or a sharp fall in overpriced stocks.

"*Devil take the hindmost*", "*sauve qui peut*"(every man for himself), "*die Letzen beissen die Hunde*" (dogs bite the laggards) and the like are signals of a panic. Bankruptcies multiply and houses of cards collapse.

The Germans fittingly name it *Torschlusspanik*, "door-closing-panic", as people bunch up to get through the doors before these slam shut. Not nearly everyone can get in.

In tune with the growing over-indebtedness of banks, companies, and citizens, one country after another fell into financial distress from 2007 onward. An open crisis and economic downturn followed, with Greece, Iceland, Ireland and Portugal as the most hard-hit victims. In due course, perhaps even Spain may be in danger of appearing on this "hit list".

Commercial and financial crises are intimately bound up with transactions that overstep the confines of law, regulations and morality, even if these confines are often shadowy. The inclination to swindle or to be swindled runs hand in hand with the inclination to speculate during a boom.

Crashes and panics, with their motto "every man for himself", encourage even more people to cheat in order to save themselves. The signal for stampedes is also sometimes connected with the revelation of major frauds.

In the 1700s, Daniel Defoe aptly compared different crimes. He thought that the stockjobber's cheating was "ten thousand times worse" than the highwayman's, because the jobber robbed people he knew and ran no physical "*risque*". Certainly Defoe would have denounced today's pyramid swindlers much more sternly than he did his stockjobbers.

Are there countries where speculation is more likely than in others? The United States seems to be the classic centre of commercial and financial panics, partly due to a tradition of wildcat banking and reckless investing, as witnessed recently by the banking crisis.

The engines for this speculative urge may lie in the extreme dynamism of the US economy, coupled with permissive supervisory institutions, especially after Reaganism reinvented the *laissez-faire* policy in the 1980s. The decade of the 1920s in the United States has been called "the greatest era of crooked high finance the world has ever known".

But the last half of the 1990s and the early 2000s also produced a bumper crop of scams, swindles and frauds.

Great Britain also offers many examples of panics and manias, from the South Sea Bubble to the Railway Mania in the 1840s, the post-World War I boom and the IT boom in the 1990s. Some observers see Britain as a country in which a spirit of adventurism and speculation has promoted crises and depressions, as reflected in the widespread betting mania.

Ivar Kreuger was estimated to have embezzled some $250 million (almost $4 billion today) in the 1920s and early 1930s. According to *White-Collar Crime*, that was about two thousand times more than the loot of the United States' public enemies number one to six, who gained only a measly $130,000 through burglary and robbery in 1938.

Two Types of Swindlers

The swindlers presented in this book may be classified into two distinct groups: those who started their working life in an honest way, and those who, from their early youth, embarked upon swindling.

In the first group we find Ivar Kreuger. During his early highly successful professional career as a construction engineer, there are no reports of his doing anything morally untoward. Kreuger's offences started only when his worldwide match empire ran afoul in the wake of Black Thursday and the stock market crash in 1929.

Bernard Cornfeld may also be included in this reputable group at the beginning of his career, before the International Overseas Services conglomerate faced serious financial problems in the volatile stock market environment of the 1960s.

Probably yet another Bernard, but with the family name Madoff, started off his career as a dealer/broker in an honest way, before he embarked on his world-record swindling operations. Perhaps even the infamous General Gregor MacGregor could be included in this group, as could CEO Kenneth Lay of Enron before he started his wheeling and dealing.

However, the other Top 10 swindlers such as Victor Lustig, not to mention Charles Ponzi, Robert Vesco and WinCapita's CEO Hannu Kailajärvi, started their frauds rather early in their lives.

From here onward the reader will be able to follow the fascinating life stories of all these men, their lust for money, the speculation, the gimmicks, the impoverishment of their victims and the colourful history of money swindling from the early days until today.

THE SPECTACULAR
SOUTH SEA BUBBLE

Chancellor of the Exchequer (that is, finance minister) Robert Harley, first Earl of Oxford, founded the South Sea Company in London in 1711. The general idea was to create a successful foreign trade company, whose profits could be used to repay the debts of the British army and navy and stabilise the public debt situation. The government's borrowing had led to a debt burden of £10 million (almost £1.4 billion today).

The South Sea bubble was closely linked to the privatisation of this huge state debt. Some prominent merchants took the debt upon themselves within the framework of the company. The *quid pro quo* was that the holders of the state bonds would gradually exchange, that is, convert, their state bonds into shares in the South Sea Company.

The chancellor was very proud of his role in the project. His flatterers named it "The Earl of Oxford's masterpiece", according to Charles McKay. Each year the company received a six per cent interest rate subsidy from the government, in order to be able to pay the annual interest of £600,000 for the state debt to the banks.

Because of this, the South Sea Company was granted a monopoly in trading with the South Seas' Spanish colonies in South America. To finance its interest rate subsidy to the company, the British Government imposed permanent import duties on many desirable colonial goods, such as wines, vinegar, India goods, wrought silks, tobacco, whale fins and some other articles.

The company's management bragged publicly about the huge riches in South America. It was widely believed that the fabulous gold and silver mines in Peru and Mexico were inexhaustible – and the company only needed to export fine British products to be paid a hundredfold in gold and silver ingots by the natives.

Public opinion was one of excitement when the rumour went around that Spain had agreed to open up four ports on the coasts of Chile and Peru for British merchant vessels. Investor interest in the shares of the South Sea

Company spread like wildfire and was fanned for several years to come – although King Philip V of Spain had no intention whatsoever of opening such free trade for the country's British competitors.

After tedious negotiations the company received exclusive rights to sell black slaves in South America for the next 30 years. But on the import side, only one single medium-sized British ship a year was allowed to trade with Mexico, Chile and Peru – and even then on the condition that Philip V received one fourth of the profits, and a tax of five per cent on the remainder.

The Main Culprit John Blunt

John Blunt was elected chairman of the board of the South Sea Company. He was dutifully assisted by the sly company treasurer, Robert Knight. Blunt was a founding director of the company and the leading figure behind the debt conversion scheme.

Blunt was the son of a shoemaker, and a Baptist by religion. His original profession was a scrivener. According to Edward Chancellor in his book, *Devil Take the Hindmost*, Blunt was a disagreeable character: burly, overbearing, glib, ingenious and with a strong desire to rise in society.

Blunt held the view that people should not know too much about the affairs of the company: the more confusion, the better. Since the conversion of the state debt into company shares was particularly advantageous for the South Sea Company, he promoted it decisively in order to expedite the rise of its share price. His main objective was to enrich himself through all means, whether legal or illegal.

The company sailed before the wind and already in 1717 its share capital was increased from £10 million to £12 million. This exceptionally large share issue to the general public was completed in cold blood although the much hyped trade with South America hardly produced any income for the company.

The South Sea Company's success was further boosted by donating shares to a number of prominent people – even to King George I and his court and, of course, to many government ministers and members of parliament – who right away started to back the company in different ways. Amassing personal riches was much more interesting to them than dampening any excesses on the stock exchange.

In parliament, Robert Walpole, a statesman, the finance minister after 1721 and later the prime minister, strongly opposed the excessive and unscrupulous support extended to the company. He warned that the company would fail, "which would lead to general discontent and ruin upon the country".

But the company's most vehement backer, finance minister John Aislabie, who had a huge personal interest in it, prevailed. Walpole was labelled a "false prophet", a Cassandra predicting all tragedies.

Raging Speculation on the London Stock Exchange

The atmosphere on the London Stock Exchange at Exchange Alley was feverish with excitement. The share price of the South Sea Company had more than doubled, from £130 to £300 per share in the spring of 1720. The directors, and especially board chairman John Blunt, did everything in their power to manipulate the share price upwards.

Blunt even stated publicly that the company would be the richest the world ever saw, and that every £100 invested would produce hundreds of pounds each year to the stockholder.

Additional share issues on easy terms were spurred on by the company demanding only a 20 per cent cash deposit against the purchase of shares. Buyers were given plenty of time – 16 months – to pay for the rest of their share purchases.

The company also offered generous loans to shareholders against the shares as deposit. These loans were financed with new share issues, which meant that money flowed in through one door and out another. The exclusive aim of the management was to boost the share price for their personal benefit.

The general impression was that the whole nation had turned into stockjobbers. Crowds blocked the Exchange Alley, and it was impossible to traverse London City's Cornhill Street due to the traffic jams caused by the innumerable horse carriages. "Every fool aspired to be a knave", was how a common joke ran, according to Charles McKay.

Other Speculative Bubble Companies

In the wake of the South Sea Company steaming ahead under the special protection of the government, a great number of imaginative new bubble companies saw the light of day. Their main purpose was to fleece the public, after which they disappeared like smoke in the air with their loot. Almost all of these companies were built on sand, a kind of financial alchemy.

One of the legendary bubble companies was established for "carrying on an undertaking of great advantage but no one to know what it is". The sales prospectus stated that the required capital was £500,000, divided into five thousand shares of £100 each.

The deposit to be paid by each subscriber was minor, only £2 per share. Having made this initial payment, each participant would be entitled to £100 in profits each year per share. The issuer promised to announce full particulars about the company in a month's time, when the remaining £98 per share was to be paid.

At nine in the morning, following the announcement, the founder of the company opened an office at Cornhill. The doorway was blocked by people who rushed in to buy shares in the company. When the office closed at three in the afternoon, one thousand shares had been subscribed and the deposits paid.

In only six hours the founder had collected £2,000, a sum equivalent to many years' salary. He settled for this and fled to the European continent with his loot. He was never heard of again.

Other bubble companies were established for the collection and sale of human hair, for insuring and increasing children's fortunes and "For a Wheel for Perpetual Motion". One company in the field of alchemy proposed to extract silver from lead. Another was created to garner large volumes of saltpetre by emptying all the "necessary houses", that is lavatories, everywhere in England.

A further sales prospectus was circulated on the Stock Exchange, proposing to raise money for a company "to drain the Red Sea, in search of the gold and jewels left by the Egyptians in their passage after the Israelites". One man presented a strange invention, an air pump for invigorating the human brain.

Only four of the 190 new bubble companies founded in 1720 survived. Two of those were insurance companies, the Royal Exchange and the London Assurance, which later flourished.

Most bubble companies preyed on the credulity and cynicism of those who bought their shares, according to Edward Chancellor. Some speculators did not buy bubble company shares as long-term investments, but with the intention to sell them shortly at a good profit to greater fools.

Very soon they discovered that there were no greater fools in the market than themselves.

The Share Price Peaks and Blunt Knighted

To accelerate the rise in the share price further, the corrupt board of the company decided to pay out a princely "midsummer dividend" of ten per cent in 1720. Chairman Blunt had of course anticipated this splendid business gift by buying call options on the midsummer dividend.

Shocked by the madness in the stock markets, the Dutch banker, Crellius, exclaimed in 1720 that Exchange Alley in London "resembled nothing so much as if all the Lunatics had escaped out of the Madhouse at once".

With the aim of monopolising as much of the speculative money as possible for his South Sea Company, John Blunt persuaded his friends in the government and parliament to approve the Bubble Act. It made it illegal to establish companies without parliamentary permission. For good measure, it prevented existing companies from carrying on activities not specified in their charters.

On the very same day, 9 June 1720, as the Bubble Act was approved in parliament, John Blunt received a baronetcy from King George I – who himself had substantial interests in the South Sea Company.

A couple of weeks later, the company announced that the year's dividend would be a whopping 30 per cent, that is, £30 on the nominal share value of £100. At the same time, the company ventured to state that it guaranteed a 50 per cent annual dividend for the 12 years ahead.

By May 1720 the management had succeeded in pumping up the share price to £500. A full two-thirds of the holders of the state debt had exchanged – that is, privatised – their safe, gilt-edged government bonds into the risky stocks of the South Sea Company.

In early June the stock price almost exploded, shooting up to nearly £900. At that moment many investors, especially within the king's court and the associated high society, came to their senses and decided to realise their profits by selling their shares.

Thomas Guy, a miserly stationer who had amassed a fortune buying sailors' tickets (credit notes issued by the mighty navy in lieu of pay) at steep discounts, sold his shares early. They had initially cost him £54,000 and the sale price was a staggering £234,000.

Guy later repented his life of avarice. He used part of his fortune to endow the hospital that bears his name. It is the prestigious and large Guy's Hospital in the centre of London.

Fatal Mistakes by Isaac Newton and King George I

The renowned Sir Isaac Newton, one of the foremost scientific intellects of all time, was Master of the Mint at the time. He also decided to sell his valuable shares in the South Sea Company for £7,000. However, having collected his large profit, he soon changed his mind and made a sizeable new investment in the company, after the shares had already peaked. As their value collapsed, he lost a large sum of money, £20,000 pounds (almost £3 million today).

The bitter loss irked Newton so much that when somebody asked his advice regarding the stock market, his answer was: "I can calculate the motions of the heavenly bodies, but not the madness of the people."

In June 1720 the Chancellor of the Exchequer, John Aislabie, tried to convince King George I to sell his South Sea stocks at the prevailing peak price. The greedy king ignored the advice and sold only a few shares to raise enough cash to purchase even more shares in the new stock issue. The story does not tell at which sale price the king finally got rid of his shares.

With the king leading the way, the people followed. On 24 August 1720, the company launched a sky-high fourth share issue for the formidable sum of £75 million. In order to sustain the stock rally, the company granted loans of over £12 million to buyers of South Sea stocks. They could even be used as security for the loans.

The Share Price Collapse Causes Suicide Wave

Late in the summer of 1720, the share collapsed as many big shareholders sold their stocks. The board members made massive support purchases in order to stabilise the price, and it recovered for a short period to a peak of £1,050. In less than six months the share had thus risen eight times.

However, the secret leaked out that the chairman of the company, the brand new Baron Blunt, and some other members of the company board had sold their shares. As a result, the stock price fell to £700.

With the money that he had collected through his massive share sales, Blunt started to buy landholdings for himself. Actually, he even sold more shares than he owned because he was convinced that after some time, he would be able to buy the shares he didn't actually have at a lower price.

Prominent foreign investors, including the canton of Bern in Switzerland, sold their share positions and repatriated their profits. In an effort to stabilise the share price, Blunt instructed every board member to purchase South Sea Company shares for a few thousand pounds. Yet the old fox himself did not follow his own decree: he bought only a minimum himself.

In mid-September, the share dropped even more steeply to £400, as quite a few investors who had bought worthless bubble company shares on credit were forced to sell their South Sea shares in order to cover their debts. Besides, few people trusted Blunt's promise that the company would be able to pay a 50 per cent dividend in the next few years.

In the early autumn the company had used up all available support measures for the stock, and there was no positive news about the company's business. Lacking steering power, the company inevitably saw the collapse of its share price.

The bankruptcy of the Sword Blade Bank dealt another serious blow. It had acted as the house bank of the company, and made the basic mistake of granting huge amounts of loans with gradually "devalued" South Sea Company shares as collateral. At the end of September, the stock price had drifted down to £200, having fallen by a hair-raising 75 to 80 per cent in four weeks.

Hundreds of ruined investors committed suicide, thousands were bankrupted. Even more of them turned into beggars. Alerted by this financial and human tragedy, King George I and his entourage returned swiftly from Hannover and parliament was called into session.

At a meeting of the South Sea Company, a shareholder declared that with ruin so widespread, it had "almost become unfashionable not to be bankrupt".

In parliament, Robert Walpole reminded the members about his stern warnings, stressing that, as he had suspected, the great bubble had now burst. The thousands of families swept into dire poverty now clamoured for heavy punishment for the company board and for Baron Blunt in particular.

The most vehement speaker in parliament was Lord Molesworth, an Irish member, who, according to Edward Chancellor, declared:

"Extraordinary crimes call for extraordinary remedies. The Roman lawgivers had not foreseen the possible existence of parricide. But as soon as the first monster appeared he was sewn in a sack and cast headlong in the river; and I shall be content to inflict the same treatment on the authors of our present ruin."

Evidently the good Lord thought that the Thames would be a most suitable place for this purpose.

The Culprits Arrested or Escaped

Official investigations revealed that Chancellor of the Exchequer John Aislabie had received large numbers of shares as a gift. He was forced to resign from the government.

Chairman Blunt and five other board members were jailed in the dreary Tower prison, accused of serious fraud and breach of trust. The general view was that, from the very start, Blunt was the author and perpetrator of the enormous scam.

Not all offenders were caught though. The notorious company treasurer, Robert Knight, managed to escape. In the darkness of the night he embarked in disguise on a small boat on the river and proceeded to Calais in France. In addition to carrying a fair supply of money with him, he travelled with his account books and other secret company documents. In view of his important accessory role in the swindle, a princely reward of £2,000 was offered for the arrest of Knight in a decree signed by the king himself.

In the parliamentary hearings Blunt had already managed to "forget" most company matters or refused to comment on them. However, it was proved that among his many other offences, the company under his leadership had created a large number of fictive shares.

Because these shares did not exist in reality and because no price or subscription fees had been paid for them as they were donated to government ministers, parliamentarians and high officials, to me these shares represented a type of share option: when the share price rose, the holders could cash in their profits.

The bribes were exceedingly generous, from £10,000 to £250,000 (some £35 million today), depending on the position and the influence of the person.

Needless to say, the receivers of such magnanimous gifts had a strong interest in promoting the company by all means possible to support a rapid rise in the price of their shares.

The Day of Reckoning

The directors of the South Sea Company received severe sentences, even if none of them was sewn into a sack and thrown into the Thames, as Lord Molesworth had wished. Immense assets were confiscated from their estates, altogether about £2 million (this sum can be compared with the total government debt of £10 million in 1711). They were left with only very little money, depending on the extent of their guilt.

The main offender Blunt was allowed to keep a scanty £5,000, only some three per cent of his total assets worth about £183,000. Other guilty persons could retain slightly more, mostly £10,000. Compared with their past standard of living, this sum meant that they joined the ranks of the poor for the rest of their lives.

Chancellor Aislabie, who was rightly branded as the other major offender alongside Blunt, was also punished harshly. Besides being expelled from parliament and thrown in jail, his gigantic bank account of £800,000 (some £110 million today) was confiscated and distributed to the victims of the South Sea bubble.

Some major stock speculators lost almost incredible sums of money. Sir Justus Beck, a director of the Bank of England, went bankrupt for £347,000. The seriously rich Duke of Sandos had to say goodbye to £700,000 of his fortune.

Rational Bubbles and Momentum Investing

With the benefit of hindsight, we see that most of the shareholders of the South Sea Company behaved thoughtlessly, as Edward Chancellor points out. Firstly, after the share price had risen sharply, there was enough public information hinting that the share was heavily overpriced. Secondly, those who bought shares after the price had already risen steeply could hope for only very limited upside at great risk. Thirdly, the company's long-term outlook had not changed much during 1720, and there was no real economic reason for the surge in the stock price.

The Swiss and Dutch professional investors and the rich London merchants did better than the average investor, because they sold their shares in good time.

The so-called rational bubble theory, which attempts to explain stock market speculation, does not seem to be anything other than the "greater fool" investment strategy. It proposes that speculators deliberately buy overpriced stocks in the hope that some fool (the greater one) will be willing to pay even more for them before the bubble bursts.

The adherents of the rational bubble theory do not recognise that its strategic applicability totally depends on the liquidity of the equity markets, that both buyers and sellers are still active in the markets. In a crisis situation the buyers may, however, withdraw from the markets at the very moment when those who swear by the rational bubble theory would wish to sell their shares.

The greater fool method became quite popular in the United States in the booming stock markets of the 1990s. It was even renamed "momentum investing", meaning, rapidly adapting to changing circumstances in the stock markets.

Momentum investors buy stocks which appear to rise faster than the stock markets and sell them as the upward movement seems to subside. The excessive short-term fluctuations in the prices of many stocks are largely due to the popularity of momentum investing.

Thus many investors in the South Sea stocks tried almost three hundred years ago to apply the principles of momentum investing, even if the majority sold their stocks too late, after the price had already dropped sharply, ultimately to only 15 per cent of its peak valuation.

Although thousands of investors lost their fortunes and, naturally, their trust in investing, the downturn which followed the South Sea bubble was neither long nor deep. The bankruptcies of British companies (with the exception of the pure bubble companies) did not spread widely during 1721, and the economy gradually recovered.

The Bubble Remembered Until the Great Railway Mania

In stock market circles the South Sea bubble was remembered for a long time. It took over one hundred years before England saw its next huge speculative wave, the Great Railway Mania in 1845–1946.

It followed the usual pattern: at the outset, the Industrial Revolution had created a great deal of prosperity, including a much richer middle class. The railway heralded a new era as it could transport both freight and people efficiently and cheaply.

A railway network which covered the whole country opened up completely new vistas for developing Great Britain. Therefore, the stocks of various railway companies rose in a spectacular manner, as common investors and large speculators increased their stakes.

The railway mania peaked in 1846. The primary victims of the excessive optimism were those middle-class families who had invested a large part or all of their savings into the shares of the foundering railway companies. They lost millions in the face of the equity collapse and the inevitable bankruptcies. The situation is to some extent reminiscent of the IT boom some 150 years later, in the 1990s.

INVENTOR OF THE PHANTOM STATE OF POYAIS, GENERAL GREGOR MACGREGOR

The swindling career of the "president" of the phantom state of Poyais, General Gregor MacGregor, seems almost inconceivable at first. But there is some written evidence, primarily in English newspapers in the 1820s, substantiating the scam – even if the various versions, as always in similar cases of swindles, differ somewhat.

It all started in 1820, when the brave General MacGregor led a small military reconnaissance patrol from Venezuela to the Gulf of Honduras. The dirt-poor swampland region was known as the Mosquito Shore, in line with the name of the local tribe. The specific area in the Caribbean was called the territory of Poyais.

Actually, it had already become a British protectorate in 1655. However, its few European settlers had left the place soon afterwards, terribly disappointed. But now the local Indian chieftain, "King" George Frederic Augustus I, agreed after some soft persuasion to make a sizeable land grant to MacGregor, enabling him to sell land rights to new European settlers in the coastal area.

Gregor MacGregor was born in 1786 in Edinburgh, the son of Captain Daniel MacGregor and his wife Ann Austin. He joined the British navy in 1803, at the age of 17. In accordance with a common custom of the time, he also served as a mercenary elsewhere, in the Spanish and Portuguese armies, and returned to Edinburgh in 1810.

The Venezuelan independence hero, Simon Bolivar, visited London in 1811 to solicit help in his fight against the Spaniards. Having learnt about the visit, MacGregor, who had adapted well to military life and was adventurous, saw his chance. He volunteered to join Bolivar's army.

When MacGregor arrived in Caracas, he was placed under the command of General Francisco de Miranda. It was assumed that MacGregor learnt about Miranda's dream of creating a new Inca state, which perhaps gave him the idea to establish his own "state".

General Miranda defected to the Spaniards, but was jailed and died in the Cadiz jail. MacGregor remained loyal to Bolivar and played an important role in Bolivar's victory over the Spaniards at Araure, west of Caracas. He was rewarded for bravery and promoted to a general in Bolivar's army.

The Prince of Poyais Arrives in London

The British economy prospered after the war against Napoleon, with the victory at Waterloo as its climax in 1815. Britain ruled the waves and had vast and rich colonies.

Many British had made great profits on the London Stock Exchange, led by the Rothschilds. Wars stimulated the markets, as seen many times later. A French saying goes like this: *"Achétez aux canons, vendez aux clarions"* ("Buy at the cannons' roar, sell when the trumpets sound"). After the first scare following the outbreak of war, stocks could often be bought cheaply, and later sold at a high price after peace was secured, like after Waterloo.

The Industrial Revolution in Britain was gradually starting. London had emerged as the leading banking centre of the world, and money was flowing everywhere. British merchants were all too eager to enter the South American market that Spain had denied them.

Unexpectedly, His Royal Highness, the Cazique of Poyais, arrived in London in 1821. Cazique is the title of chieftains in the Indian areas of South America's Spanish regions, and is equivalent to prince.

The prince who appeared in London was, however, not a genuine prince by birth. His Highness the Cazique of Poyais was originally a Scottish soldier, and his name was Gregor MacGregor. This adventurer and colonial conqueror had simply obtained the title of an Indian prince through his horse trading with the local ruler, George Frederic Augustus I.

MacGregor used the name, Principality of Poyais, for his fief. It was the place which he had visited as leader of his expedition. The principality comprised 32,400 square kilometres.

MacGregor skilfully exploited both the tremendous interest in investing money in almost any type of project, and the public's ignorance about the outside world. It was not well known, especially not distant Central America.

Before long, MacGregor's new and even more impressive official title was elevated to Gregor I. In his boastful tales, Poyais' dirt-poor, sunburnt end of the world was portrayed as a paradise, surrounded by lofty, gold-rich mountains. Mahogany and cedar trees were said to be growing everywhere, and the fertile land provided excellent pasture for large livestock. In Poyais, so he recounted, practically any type of plant thrived, including cotton, sugar cane, corn and tropical fruits.

Gregor I's publicity stunts also announced that the country's capital housed a parliament, palaces, an opera house, a cathedral, boulevards, bridges, banks and a busy harbour. It was located on the mouth of the Black River, which flowed through Poyais.

The government was reportedly democratic. The parliament had, strangely enough, three chambers. The head of state was, of course, Gregor I.

These spectacular stories were not at all questioned. Nobody cared to ask if somebody in London's Whitehall, the centre of the British Government, or in the British navy or the commercial marine, had heard of Poyais.

On his part, Gregor I did not allow much time for anyone to check the facts. His stories were perhaps trusted also because he was a colourful general, who vividly recalled his victorious battles in South America. Accompanied by his Spanish-American wife, Josefa, he was well received in London's high society.

For example, in 1822 the Mayor of London, Christopher Magnay, gave an official grand reception in honour of Gregor I in the City of London's ceremonial and administrative town hall, the monumental Guildhall.

Advertising the Wonders of the Phantom State

In London, Gregor I was introduced to Major William John Richardson. Before long, Richardson was appointed envoy of Poyais. Even King George IV received Richardson in official audience. The diplomatic recognition of Poyais probably took place with the help of some discreet bribes.

The energetic MacGregor soon published a full 350-page guidebook on his country. The name of the book was *Sketch of the Mosquito Shore, including the Territory of Poyais*. Its purported author was a certain captain with the peculiar name of Thomas Strangeways. Later it was suspected that the book had been written by a ghost writer – that is, the very same head of state, Gregor I.

In the guidebook, Poyais was pictured in an exceptionally favourable light. It was emphasised that English settlers had already founded St. Joseph, the capital of Poyais, in the 1730s. Therefore, Poyais was a particularly anglophile country, with well-developed infrastructure (roads and harbours), untapped gold and silver mines, and fertile lands which only awaited their settlers.

In particular, the book pointed out the enormous profits guaranteed by the country's rich natural resources. To crown it all, readers were assured that the region was free of tropical diseases – indeed an amazing statement for a place the name of which, after all, was the Mosquito Shore!

As befitted his high station, Gregor I moved to the splendid Oak Hall in Essex, which was owned by his envoy Richardson. The legation of Poyais was inaugurated in the City of London at Dowgate Hill. Side offices of the legation were opened in Edinburgh and Glasgow.

The head of state of Poyais further cemented his standing by hosting several elaborate banquets at Oak Hall. Among the dignitaries invited were government ministers, foreign ambassadors and senior military officers.

Land Rights for Sale and Loan from the City

The settlement project for Poyais started off in Edinburgh, MacGregor's hometown. He sold land rights in Poyais, at first for slightly over three and later, four shillings per acre. The initial price equalled about £40 per square kilometre.

The price looked quite favourable. A worker's salary in those days was about £1 a week, with which it was possible to buy about five to six acres of the advertised fertile land.

Land rights were sold in rapidly growing numbers because many people wanted to start a new life in a new country. The transactions were generally made in the presence of whole families.

The energetic Gregor I struck when the iron was hot. On behalf of the Poyais government, he was able to raise a huge loan from the public. The loan sum was £200,000 (almost £15 million today), and the intermediary in this transaction was a bank in the affluent City of London. The purpose of the loan was stated as "stabilising the state finances of Poyais".

The loan was set up in the form of bearer bonds sold to the public and yielding six per cent interest per annum to the bond holders. The nominal value of the 2,000 bonds was £100 per bond.

The loan was managed by the London banker, Sir John Sperring. Strangely enough this experienced banker did not question why the loan was secured only by the "general resources of the state of Poyais", a completely unknown factor in banking circles. His credulity may have been due to the fact that King George IV had given his blessing to the project by receiving the envoy of Poyais, Major Richardson.

As the interest rate of the bonds was tempting, the bonds were eagerly subscribed by unsuspecting investors. It was sold out in a short time, after which the money was passed on to the bank account of Gregor I.

The First Victims Leave

Next, from word to deed. The Poyais legation chartered the ship *Honduras Packet,* whose crew knew MacGregor from earlier days. They could keep their mouths shut. Five London merchants received contracts to provision this and later ships with food and ammunition.

The ship departed from the port of London in September 1822 with 70 passengers, among them a doctor, a lawyer and a banker, who had been promised a suitable post in the state administration of Poyais. A few passengers had paid MacGregor for officers' commissions in the Poyais army.

The would-be settlers also included many farmers, who had sold their land to pay for the land rights in Poyais and the ocean-crossing. In addition, there were some craftsmen, whose work situation had deteriorated in the wake of the mass production that was part of the nascent Industrial Revolution.

The cargo also included a closely guarded strongbox full of Poyais dollars. The inventive MacGregor had had these so-called dollars printed in Scotland. Many of the passengers made the fateful mistake of exchanging their valuable British pounds for completely worthless Poyais paper-dollars.

Terrible Shock on Arrival

The arrival of the *Honduras Packet* at its destination presented a terrible shock to the passengers. All they found were empty shores, untouched jungle, sunburnt dry hills and a few natives sneaking around.

There was no sign of the imposing capital, St. Joseph. Only a few ruins on the shore, as a sad reminder of the colonisation attempt by the British in the distant past.

To make matters worse, a hurricane swept the *Honduras Packet* back to the high seas. The unfortunate first settlers found themselves shipwrecked on the shore, without dwellings or food.

The next, much larger, ship, the *Kennersley Castle*, sailed out of Leith harbour in Scotland on 22 January 1823. Food for one year had been stored for the immigrants. The ship arrived at its destination on 20 March with 200 passengers, slightly delayed as it had been looking in vain for the alleged port for two days.

The newcomers found the exhausted immigrants of the *Honduras Packet* in a dreadful state. Tropical diseases had already started to take their toll among them, and one had committed suicide. *Kennersley Castle* returned swiftly back to Scotland.

Many of the exasperated immigrants died before news about their distress reached British Honduras, hundreds of kilometres north of Poyais. A rescue ship from Belize, the *Mexican Eagle*, arrived at the last moment and saved many of the passengers from certain death.

A final disaster was still awaiting them. In the presence of King George Frederic Augustus I, Lieutenant Colonel Hector Hall, appointed future governor of Poyais, much regretted to inform the would-be settlers that the king had revoked his land grant, on which the land rights sold to the settlers were based. The reason for the turnaround was that MacGregor had declared the area to be independent.

A few British vessels went out to sea in order to intercept seven other ships on their way to Poyais, and accompany them either to nearby harbours, or direct them back to England and Scotland.

Later information revealed that more than 180 would-be settlers from the first two ships perished during the ordeal in Poyais or in the hospitals of British Honduras. More settlers died during the exhausting 72-day voyage back home. Fewer than 50 came back alive to Britain. Their ship, the *Ocean,* docked in London in October 1823.

The Sad Return to Britain

British newspapers published horrified accounts about the Poyais scandal, as outraged survivors returned home with their tails between their legs to recount their fate and seek those responsible for the swindle.

Interestingly enough, in spite of their sufferings, many survivors refused to believe that MacGregor was the main culprit. One of the travellers, James Hastie, having lost two of his children to tropical diseases, wrote a book about the voyage of *Kennersley Castle*. He blamed MacGregor's collaborators for the failure of the settlement project and the newspapers for spreading false information.

Some of the participants even signed a declaration. They were convinced that if MacGregor himself had participated in the journey, matters would have turned out differently. Major Richardson sued newspapers for libel and defended his friend MacGregor against the fraud charges.

MacGregor's Swindle Continued in France

At that stage MacGregor had already fled with his loot to France, to continue his swindle on virgin soil. He had contacted a French trading house called Compagnie de la Nouvelle Neustrie in advance, agreeing to let it have exclusive rights to market the settlement project in France.

In August 1825 MacGregor published the new constitution of Poyais. He changed it to a republic, whose self-proclaimed president he became.

La Nouvelle Neustrie started recruiting French settlers for Poyais on the condition that they bought shares in the company for 100 francs. News of the sad fate of the English and Scottish emigrants had not yet reached France as the information flow between England and France was slow and scant in those days.

The French officials were, however, alert. They noted that a number of people had obtained passports in order to travel to a country they had never heard of. They confiscated Nouvelle Neustrie's vessel, which lay waiting in the Le Havre harbour.

Some of the French who had enrolled and paid for the trip also realised that everything was not in order. They requested an official investigation into the activities of Nouvelle Neustrie and MacGregor.

As a result, MacGregor's friend from the army, Gustavus Butler Hippisley, and his secretary Thomas Irving, were arrested and transported to the La Force prison in Paris. MacGregor himself was in hiding. But after a couple of months he was also apprehended and placed in the same prison. Somewhat later the prisoners were transferred to the Parisian Bicetre prison.

The trial began on 6 April 1826. With the help of his top-class defence lawyer, Morilhou, MacGregor was acquitted in July 1826. Hippisley and Irving were also released. However, Monsieur Lehuby, who was one of the directors of La Nouvelle Neustrie, was sentenced to 13 months in jail for making false promises.

The Not-so-Grand Finale

When the furore over these affairs had died down, the daring MacGregor returned to London. He was arrested shortly after his arrival and taken to the Bridewell prison in Tothill Fields in London's Westminster district. He was released in less than a week.

The general opened up a new Poyais office at 23 Threadneedle Street, close to the Bank of England, located on the same street. Once again, he tried to raise a substantial loan, but investors were now alerted to the "Poyais humbug" and the loan project failed utterly.

MacGregor returned to Scotland in 1834. There he had to sign new land rights for Poyais as security for the expired and unredeemed bonds. In practice, these papers were completely worthless.

Little by little MacGregor ran out of money. He was permitted to return to Venezuela in 1839, where he requested and received a general's pension, as a distinguished veteran of the war of liberation.

MacGregor died poor in Caracas in December 1845.

VICTOR LUSTIG SOLD
THE EIFFEL TOWER

Victor Lustig, or "Count von Lustig" as he preferred to call himself, was definitely one of the most shameless, but at the same time, the most inventive personalities in the history of swindles.

Victor Lustig was born in 1890, the son of the mayor in the small Czech town of Hostinne. The charming young man was sent to a private boarding school in Dresden. As a talented pupil he became fluent in several foreign languages, including German, English and later French.

When he finished school, Lustig's parents sent him for further studies in Paris. But to sustain his extravagant lifestyle he turned instead to gambling. Lustig became an accomplished poker, bridge and billiard player. His life as a swindler got off to a good start on the great Atlantic Ocean liners steaming between France and the United States. He cheated other passengers, especially rich Americans, at the gaming tables.

Lustig's criminal career was long and colourful. Having commenced as a card shark, he continued with a rudimentary money-printing machine, sold the Eiffel Tower to a Parisian scrap merchant and even cheated the infamous Al Capone.

The life of a busy fraudster such as Lustig was no dance on roses. And although he swiped millions of dollars from his victims, he squandered the money rapidly, in the same fashion as most other criminals. Lustig also earned many prison sentences, but always reverted back to his risky profession.

Crooks of Lustig's ilk try to bolster their low self-esteem with snobbish appearances and heavy spending by flashing big banknotes. This blind waste of money reflects their urge to experience and show off something great, to enjoy life and liberty to the fullest. Dirty money burns in the pockets of criminals.

The Mysterious Money-Printing Machine

Victor Lustig's first big time swindle took place in the early 1920s with a primitive "money-printing machine". The scene of the sting was Florida's affluent Palm Beach – a town where world-record swindler Bernard Madoff's most rewarding hunting grounds were located more than 80 years later.

The always immaculately dressed Lustig introduced himself locally as a European millionaire. He cruised around town in a stylish silver-grey Rolls Royce driven by a uniformed Japanese chauffeur. The car was of course rented.

Lustig did his own "market research" in this millionaires' paradise and got to know some people in the luxury hotels. One evening, while sitting in the bar of a plush hotel, he learnt that the Californian millionaire, Hermann Loller, who was in town, had just run into serious financial problems.

Inspired by this valuable intelligence, Lustig introduced himself to Loller in the breakfast room as an Austrian count, who after World War I mourned the loss of his vast landholdings. In a roundabout way, he intimated that he knew how dollar bills could be replicated.

Loller could, of course, not imagine that Lustig was aware of his financial distress. Discreetly he started to ferret out more information. After a while the fake count admitted that he was the owner of an apparatus which could copy real banknotes in a completely lifelike way.

Soon the two gentlemen moved over to Lustig's hotel suite. There Lustig showed Loller a mysterious box, which had two narrow slots on both sides. He adjusted the buttons, turned on the switches and fed a hundred-dollar bill into one of the slots, followed by an empty slip of paper. After this he explained that the copying process would take about six hours.

Six hours later, the two gentlemen returned to the suite. Lustig turned on one of the switches, and to Loller's amazement, two completely identical hundred-dollar bills popped out from the machine.

Lustig proposed to Loller that he might want to visit a bank to make sure that the forgery could not be detected. But he cautioned Loller against showing both bills in the same bank because naturally they had precisely the same serial numbers (Lustig had in advance altered the serial numbers on one of the bills, from two number threes to two eights, to make them exactly the same as on the other bill).

At this stage Loller already started dreaming about the easy money that he could make with this wonderful machine. He prayed almost on his knees that the dear count would be kind enough to sell it to him.

Lustig dug in his heels and would not listen to such a proposal. But he finally relented and reluctantly agreed to part with the miracle machine at an exorbitant price, $25,000 in cash (well over $300,000 today).

The delighted Loller left hurriedly for his bank to withdraw the necessary amount of cash. He counted out the banknotes to Lustig and headed triumphantly for his yacht, which was moored in the fashionable yacht harbour.

In the captain's cabin he opened the lid of the wonderful machine with shaking hands, in the firm belief that it would banish all his financial concerns. Inside it he found only two rubber cylinders and an empty slip of paper.

At this moment Lustig had already sped far away on the backseat of his Rolls Royce. And fearful of losing his reputation, the disgraced Loller did not have the stomach to contact the police.

Sale of the Eiffel Tower to a Parisian Scrap Merchant

Victor Lustig's chosen profession called for frequent changes of his whereabouts, partly for fear of revenge by victims, or capture by the police, and partly to seek new swindling pastures. Therefore, after a successful racetrack scam in Montreal, he left Canada for Paris in 1925.

France had already recovered from its frightful ordeal during World War I. The economy was booming, creating an opportune environment for various types of frauds.

One morning Lustig, who was fluent in French, was reading a local newspaper in a street café. A news story reported that the maintenance costs of the Eiffel Tower, which had been erected for the Paris World Fair in 1889, were so elevated that they posed an unacceptable burden on the French Government's finances. The tower had already rusted badly in places and each year the painting work cost millions of francs. On top of everything, expensive structural renovations were on the horizon.

The author of the article made a brave suggestion: that the Eiffel Tower, which even originally had not been regarded as a permanent construction, should be sold as valuable scrap metal. Instantly, Lustig came to think of a daring and intricate idea for a swindle, which he developed further with his assistant, Robert Arthur Tourbillon, whose formal title was private secretary. His other name was Dan Collins.

Lustig now turned to a top-level forger working in a printing house and asked him to print high-grade fake government stationery with the official letterhead of the Ministry of Posts and Telegraphs. In addition, he ordered business cards with his title and the name of the ministry.

After receiving the stationery he drafted an "official" letter in the name of the ministry to six well-known Parisian scrap merchants. The gentlemen were invited to an urgent and confidential meeting in Hotel Crillon, which was, and is, one of the most prestigious old hotels in Paris, located at the Place de la Concorde. The stated topic of the meeting was a possible major business deal with the French Government.

All six men arrived dutifully at the hotel at the agreed hour. On behalf of the Ministry of Posts and Telegraphs, Lustig greeted everybody and introduced himself as one of its deputy director generals – which was almost as high a position as a junior minister. The guests had been invited to the meeting as honest and reputable businessmen.

The topic of the evening was to discuss a delicate and pressing problem, which fell under the ministry's authority: the Eiffel Tower. He lamented that the upkeep of the tower was so outrageously expensive that it could not be defended any longer. The authorities were forced to sell the tower, which even when being erected had been regarded as temporary.

Lustig reminded the guests that the idea was not entirely new. There had already been plans to dismantle the tower in 1909 and to move it somewhere else. Besides the exorbitant costs for the upkeep, the ministry was of the view that such an ugly steel construction was out of harmony with the other classic attractions of Paris, such as the Notre Dame, Louvre, the Invalides church, the Arc de Triomphe and the Champs-Elysées, the deputy director general revealed confidentially.

Because the dismantling of the tower was nevertheless sure to cause a public outcry, the plan had to be kept secret until the details had been agreed on. Lustig ended his introduction by stating that on very short notice he had been assigned the task of selecting the most suitable dealer to carry out the task.

After this, the guests were taken on an inspection tour of the Eiffel Tower in a big black limousine (rented, of course). The ulterior motive of the visit was to give Lustig an opportunity to gauge which one of the businessmen was the most eager and gullible victim.

To prevent anybody from making detailed background checks, he prodded the guests to submit their bids by the following morning. Finally, he once more reminded them that the whole matter had to absolutely be treated as a state secret.

By the time the guests left Lustig already knew that he would prefer to accept the bid of one of the dealers, a businessman by the name of André Poisson. Poisson was an insecure person who obviously felt he had not yet succeeded in getting into the leading business circles in Paris.

Apparently he imagined that the Eiffel Tower deal would put him in the big league.

However, on his return home, Poisson's wife was suspicious. She wondered who this high civil servant really was, why everything was so secret, and why the deal would have to be done in such haste.

In the morning Poisson himself sounded quite apprehensive and nervous on the telephone, especially after he learned from Lustig that his bid would be approved. Private secretary Tourbillon was therefore instructed to call Poisson back urgently and invite him to a confidential bilateral meeting with the "minister" – that is, Lustig – in Hotel Crillon because the matter was of such a delicate nature that they could not meet in the ministry.

At this *tête-à-tête* meeting Lustig sought to dispel Poisson's and especially his wife's suspicions by "confessing", with a highly embarrassed air, how matters really stood: although he was a high civil servant, he did not make enough money to pursue the lifestyle he enjoyed. Therefore, he needed to find ways to supplement his income. Precisely for this reason his activities presupposed the utmost discretion.

Poisson immediately got the message. He was only dealing with another corrupt government official who was after a bribe! In a split second all his doubts vanished: in the past he had made many deals with similar corrupt officials, and he had never experienced any problems with these people.

Within a couple of hours, Lustig received on behalf of the Ministry a suitcase full of cash from Poisson. Not only for the Eiffel Tower deal, the payment of which was acknowledged with an official receipt, typed on the ministry's letterhead, but also a generous personal bribe.

Carrying their huge spoils in the suitcase, Lustig and Tourbillon jumped on the first train to Vienna – in first class, of course. As Lustig had anticipated, nothing alarming was heard from Paris because Poisson was far too ashamed to turn to the police.

Allegedly, Lustig returned a little later to Paris to try to sell the Tower once more, following the same scenario as earlier on. This time the chosen victim went to the police before the deal could be closed, but the two swindlers, Lustig and Tourbillon, managed to evade arrest.

Even Al Capone Cheated

One of Lustig's most surprising targets was the notorious Chicago gangster, Al Capone himself. At the same time Lustig wanted to get to know the illustrious racketeer, with a view to possible fruitful cooperation in the future.

Lustig got wind of the location of Capone's home, which was in the Hawthorne Inn area of Chicago. Having found the right place, he loitered in front of the house protected by thick shutters. Suddenly Capone's bodyguards noticed the stranger, rushed out, dragged him into the house, frisked him and accompanied him to their master.

As a stylish gentleman Lustig made quite an impression on Capone. Lustig confided that the reason for his Chicago visit was that he planned an interesting swindle operation on Wall Street. He could guarantee that each participant would double their money in 50 days.

Having reflected on the proposal, Capone said that he would wager $50,000 (close to $800,000 today) on a scheme which sounded so profitable. He counted out the dollar bills on the table. But in the same instant he pushed a red button on his desk. The wall panel slid aside and from behind it emerged one of Capone's bodyguards, who had the looks of a killer and was armed with a submachine gun.

Lustig in fact did not have any ready-made fraud planned, although he had bragged about it in front of Capone. When he returned from Chicago to New York on the train, he was in low spirits because he knew that he was inviting disaster once and for all if he lost Capone's money. If so, he might just as well consider himself a dead man.

After the agreed time Lustig informed Capone that he would return to Chicago. In front of the desk he pretended to be extremely ashamed and told Capone in a miserable voice that the plan had not worked out, due to unexpected difficulties.

According to Lustig's own account Capone went raving mad, shouted that his money had been lost and started slowly to reach for the red button on the desk. Lustig, however, steadied his nerves and counted out all the $50,000 he had received from Capone and put them on the table, apologising once more. He said that he certainly would have wanted to earn some big money for the great Al Capone. Now everything had gone wrong, and he himself was in urgent need of money.

Capone calmed down and asked if Lustig was really broke. As he nodded, Capone gave him an open-handed gift of $5,000 and asked if that would help.

With tears in his eyes, Lustig theatrically thanked Capone, calling him a great gentleman, bowed, put the money into his wallet and left. And so one of the many stories Lustig recounted during his old-age retirement in prison ended luckily for him.

Risky Money Counterfeiting

From then onward, things went downhill for the master swindler. Lustig's cooperation with Capone's gang continued for several years and got him mixed up in a new type of hard-core crime which he had evaded in the past: large-scale money counterfeiting.

This crime field was extremely risky because its practitioners were among the main targets of the Federal Bureau of Investigation (FBI). In those days, a large part of all payments were made in cash, and therefore banknote forgery undermined the public's confidence in the dollar as a means of payment – and above all it caused much political hullabaloo and headline news, which was quite embarrassing for the police.

For all these reasons the Chicago police set up a special task force in 1934, whose main job was to bring Lustig and his companion from the

Capone gang, William Watts, before the court and in jail. The police was simply forced to stop the stream of professionally-made counterfeit dollar bills.

According to police estimates – which, as revealed in the trial, turned out to be gross underestimations – Lustig and Watts, with their accomplices, produced at least $100,000 in forged bank bills a month, a huge sum of money in those days.

Having wiretapped the two crooks for several months, the police finally had sufficient evidence for a big raid and arrested Lustig and Watts in late 1934. Although Lustig, as a slick operator, volunteered to reveal the location of the printing works to the police, in exchange for his own release of course, he was incarcerated in the Federal House of Detention in New York City. However, as an experienced jailbird, he succeeded in escaping in the classic way the day before his trial – using a sheet rope.

Retirement Days in Alcatraz

His escape took him to Pittsburgh, where Victor Lustig's new identity was a quiet pensioner, Robert V. Miller. But it was his fate to be detected, and after only 27 days of liberty he found himself behind bars again – actually his 44th prison visit during a long swindling career.

The end result of the dramatic trial was much worse than Lustig could ever have imagined. In December 1935 the Chicago tribunal found him guilty of printing and circulating the almost incredible sum of $134 million (over $2 billion today) in counterfeit bills. The sentence was 20 years in prison.

Because Lustig had quite an aggravating criminal record behind him, he was taken to the top-security island prison, Alcatraz, in San Francisco Bay. From there, not even a slippery rogue like Lustig would be able to escape.

Lustig expiated his sins in Alcatraz for over 11 years. Having contracted pneumonia, he was taken to the Medical Center for Federal Prisoners in Springfield, Missouri, where he died in March 1947.

The champion of swindlers was 57 years old.

CHARLES PONZI –
PIONEER OF PYRAMID
SCHEMES

The most widely-known large-scale swindling method, the pyramid scheme or Ponzi, derives its name from the Italian-American immigrant Charles (Carlo) Ponzi. His groundbreaking swindling technique left the name of the man permanently in the annals of financial history.

In his partially fictionalised book about Ponzi, Donald Dunn recalls that nine decades ago, Ponzi's name already invoked memories of a mammoth swindle: an ever-growing crowd of gullible citizens pouring hard-earned "investment" money into the hands of a smooth-talking individual with the promise of huge profits – after which they saw their money disappear.

Ponzi started his swindling career in 1920 in Boston, where thousands of people lost part or all of their life savings as a result of Ponzi's spectacular scam. Quite a few swindlers have since copied the idea with considerable success.

Even world-record swindler Bernard Madoff confessed at the time of his arrest that his gigantic investment fund "was just a big Ponzi".

WinCapita's suspected swindle seems to have partly copied the innovative Ponzi. At the start, investors were promised quick profits of as much as several hundred per cent. Some of them actually received these princely returns, which were in fact derived from the next investors' stakes, and not from any of the boasted super-profitable business.

New investors were lured into the scheme through personal contacts by numerous sales agents called "sponsors", who enthusiastically marketed the scheme, inspired by high commissions. Since Ponzi's time, during which there was no Internet or TV or mobile phones, the web has created enormous scope for Ponzi-type frauds in wider circles, even globally.

The Northern Italian Carlo Ponzi was born in 1882 in Lugo, close to Ravenna. As a young man he worked as a postal clerk, but soon enrolled as a student at the Sapienza university in Rome. Ponzi and his friends saw their university time as a four-year vacation. The charming young man enjoyed a carefree life and spent time with his friends in bars, cafeterias and the opera.

Ponzi may have received the first impulse for his swindling scheme from newspaper stories about William Miller. Miller was an accountant from Brooklyn in New York City. In 1899, he designed a simple pyramid scheme and raked in over a million dollars from his credulous victims. He was nicknamed "William 520 per cent Miller", in line with the exorbitant profits that he promised his investors.

Criminal Overture in Canada

Charles Ponzi arrived in Boston aboard the *S.S. Vancouver* on 15 November 1903, having gambled away his savings during the Atlantic crossing. In a later interview he told *The New York Times*: "I landed in this country with $2.50 in cash and $1 million in hopes, and those hopes never left me."

The lively Ponzi quickly learned English. In the beginning he worked in odd jobs on the East Coast, among other things, as a dishwasher in a restaurant, where he slept on the floor at the end of the working day. He gradually managed to work himself up to a waiter, but was fired for pilfering and short-changing customers' money.

In 1907 Ponzi moved to Montreal, where he started as an assistant teller in the newly opened Banco Zarossi. The bank founded by Luigi Zarossi catered to the banking needs of the influx of Italian immigrants.

Zarossi paid six per cent interest to his depositors – double the normal rate. The bank's business flourished on the strength of this financial generosity.

Ponzi soon found out that the bank was in serious trouble, due to some bad real estate loans. Zarossi financed his attractive deposit rates not through business income, but with the deposit money brought in by new clients. The bank failed, and Zarossi fled to Mexico, taking a large part of the bank's cash with him.

Ponzi stayed on in Montreal and lived in Zarossi's house for a while, helping the abandoned family. However, all the time he fantasised about returning to the land of his dreams, the United States.

Just before his departure from Montreal he fell into temptation and committed a minor cheque forgery. He was arrested and received a three-year sentence in the Quebec prison. In a letter to his mother in Italy he wrote that he worked as a special assistant to the prison warden.

Towards New Adventures in the United States

After his release in 1911, Ponzi returned to the US. There he was lured into a large-scale human-smuggling scheme, helping illegal Italian immigrants from Canada across the border. Ponzi was arrested again and sentenced to a new jail term, this time for two years in the Atlanta prison.

Within these walls he was promoted to warden's translator, as he was intercepting letters from a feared mobster, Ignazio "the Wolf" Lupo. Ponzi also met his true role model, the millionaire Charles W. Morse, who had a reputation for successful, but occasionally shady, business operations.

His friend Morse advised him to eat a lot of soap shavings, and Morse convinced the old prison doctor into believing that Ponzi was seriously ill, even dying. He was released from the Atlanta prison.

Ponzi now returned to Boston, where he married an Italian-born stenographer by the name of Rose Maria Gnecco. As evidenced by later court minutes, Ponzi did not tell Gnecco about his prison years, but his mother revealed her charming son's offences in a letter – which did not prevent the loving young girl from marrying him.

Countdown of Ponzi's Fleece

In Boston Ponzi established a small firm, which attempted to sell advertising space to various companies in a compact listing to be distributed to various businesses. Ponzi did not succeed in selling his idea widely, and the company failed.

The great swindling idea started to take form in Ponzi's head when he received a letter from Spain, in which he was asked to send a copy of his business catalogue to Spain. In the envelope was something which Ponzi had never seen before: an international postal reply coupon. He collected more information about these coupons and detected a loophole which, at least in theory, offered splendid earning possibilities.

The basic idea of the postal reply coupon was to cover postal charges in reply to a letter from abroad. It was, of course, priced according to the sender country's postal charge level, but could be exchanged for postage stamps in the addressee country for covering its own postal charges.

Ponzi noticed now that if two countries' postal charges differed from each other, it opened up a profit-making possibility. As the rampant inflation in Italy in the wake of World War I had weakened the exchange rate for the lira in relation to the US dollar – the lira had in other words been devalued against the dollar – the Italian postal charges were quite low measured in strong dollars.

Ponzi designed his pyramid marketing strategy on the basis of this idea. Its profitability was explained to prospective clients in the following manner: with the help of valuable dollars transferred to Italy, local agents would buy millions of cheap Italian international reply coupons. Those coupons would then be shipped over to the US and exchanged for higher-value American postage stamps. Finally, these stamps would be changed into cash, that is, dollars.

The scheme was actually a kind of arbitrage, profiting from price differentials in two markets. Assets would be bought cheaply elsewhere and sold in the own home market at a higher price. And best of all: it was all completely legal.

In the words of Donald Dunn, the diminutive and dapper Ponzi had a vocabulary and a manner that enabled him to captivate both the common folk of Boston's immigrant neighbourhoods and its well schooled Back Bay socialites. His scheme was simple enough on the surface to appeal to the unsophisticated, and yet intricate enough to intrigue those with financial experience.

Millions Flowing In

The plan sounded logical and attractive. The popular Ponzi invited friends and business associates to invest in the scheme by promising them a return of 50 per cent within 45 days. On a straight-line basis, that was equivalent to an annual profit of 360 per cent!

He explained to them that the high returns generated by the trade in postal reply coupons made it easy to achieve such staggering profits. To manage the business, he founded a new company with a convincing name, the Securities Exchange Company.

In his play, *Death of a Salesman*, American playwright Arthur Miller tells the story about the salesman, Willy Loman. Every morning, Loman went to work "with a smile and a shoeshine". Charles Ponzi had the same endearing smile and shine as Willy, but he offered something more: he promised quick riches to people.

Rumours about the exceptionally attractive investment spread like wildfire along the East Coast by word of mouth. Nobody cared to investigate the details of the scheme, as all and sundry trusted Ponzi's word. At first he hired dozens, and later, hundreds, of sales agents and paid them generous commissions for the dollars brought into the investment pool.

More and more investors told their friends about this "piece of cake":

$1,000 would quickly, in merely one and a half months, turn into $1,500, $10,000 into $15,000 and so forth. The initial investors were indeed paid such impressive profits, and on the strength of their praises, Ponzi gained more and more credibility every day. A frenzy was building up.

The company was flooded with money. Some of the investors were wealthy, but most were modest pension savers or even unfortunate people living close to the poverty line. They put in their last dollars in the hope of becoming rich.

Everybody trusted Ponzi. As a new charity apostle he was popularly called the "wizard of finance". In a few months' time he soared from anonymity to the status of a famous millionaire deserving of public acclaim, in an era before TV and the Internet existed to spread the word.

Some local newspapers jokingly reported that money flowed in so rapidly through doors and windows that dollar bills even had to be stowed in waste-paper baskets due to the lack of space. In actual fact every single dollar was counted and, at the end of the day, sent to a bank in which Ponzi had a controlling interest.

This bank was the Hanover Trust Bank of Boston, a small Italian-American bank on Hanover Street in the North End of Boston, populated primarily by Italian immigrants.

Within a few months, from February until July 1920, the young and inexperienced Ponzi succeeded in attracting an estimated, almost incredible, sum of $10 million with his oven-fresh company – in today's money, over $100 million. He operated his company openly and efficiently.

Many Bostonians made their investments by borrowing money from the bank against the mortgages of their houses. Or they staked their old age savings. In addition, most of those who at the early stage had raked in massive profits, reinvested those funds into Ponzi's treacherous scheme, hoping to gain even more.

The First Setbacks

The Ponzi bubble did not last very long. Even the most elementary financial analysis would have revealed that the company was losing money. As long as new "investments" continued to flow in, the money needed to pay profits to one investor came from the next two investors, and the money to pay those two came from the next four, and so on.

But the continuous new investment inflow was the only source of funds. Ponzi's firm did not generate any of the alleged business revenues. In fact he did not even bother to buy any of the postal reply coupons whose profitability he had bragged so much about.

A liquidity bomb was ticking.

Ponzi's personal finances were also strained by his extravagant lifestyle. He bought a big mansion in Lexington, Massachusetts, which boasted some features quite unusual in those days: air-conditioning and a heated swimming pool. He brought his mother from Italy to America in the first-class stateroom of one of the luxurious ocean liners. The list went on.

Gradually, more and more investors started to wonder how the 38-year-old playboy-looking Ponzi was able to rise like a comet, from a penniless bankrupt entrepreneur to a multimillionaire. Those fearing the worst hurried to cash in their profits from the Securities Exchange Company.

The reversal of the money flow was a major setback for Ponzi. He started to negotiate the sale of the company for $10 million to a New York gangster known just by the name of "Herman". The deal almost closed, but finally fell through as the Boston newspaper, *The Post*, started on 26 July 1920 to publish a series of sensational disclosures about Ponzi's life and business.

Financial Analyst Barron Smells A Rat

The scandal peaked after *The Post* hired the experienced financial analyst, Clarence Barron, of *Barron's Financial Paper*, to investigate Ponzi's business background.

To his consternation Barron discovered that Ponzi himself had not invested a single cent into his own company, despite bragging everywhere about its superior profits.

Barron's second and even more damaging observation was that, to cover the multimillion dollar investments made into the Securities Exchange Company, there ought to be more than 160 million postal reply coupons in circulation, although according to the US postal service, the actual figure was only a meagre 27,000 coupons.

The postal service also confirmed that no millions of postal reply coupons had been bought in Italy. The percentage gross profit margin from each bought and sold postal reply coupon might well be high, but the overhead costs for selling and buying these very cheap coupons (all of them had to be done individually) would have swallowed the entire imagined profit.

Investors Flee in Droves

The Post's revelations caused a run on the office of the Securities Exchange Company as investors rushed to cash in their money from the company. For three days Ponzi canvassed the boisterous crowd outside his office and personally paid out $2 million to them.

He tried to calm investors down, offering them coffee and donuts and telling them that there was no reason to be worried. Many of those present changed their minds and left their money in his care.

Little by little, the situation got worse. Investors were no longer paid anything at all. On top of everything, *The Post* published a new sensational story about Ponzi's jail sentence for his Canadian cheque forgery, adorned with a police mug shot.

The newspaper interviewed several desperate investors. In one heart-rending story, a printer from the North End sobbed that his dream of buying a new house with his $4,600 savings had now "turned into a dog-house", according to Donald Dunn.

A couple who had dreamt about returning to Italy wept over a worthless note for $2,000. A Beachmont woman who had mortgaged her house for $8,000 and invested it in Ponzi's bottomless coffers lamented, with tears in her eyes, that "not in a lifetime can I pay back that mortgage".

The funeral bells for Ponzi's pyramid were ringing. The fresh information officer of the Securities Exchange Company, James McMasters, was flabbergasted by Ponzi's endless chit-chat about postal reply coupons and the ongoing investigation. He reported to *The Post* that Ponzi was a "financial idiot".

On the basis of McMasters's information, the newspaper disclosed on 2 August 1920 that Ponzi was hopelessly insolvent. On 10 August federal agents raided the company and closed the Securities Exchange Company's office.

During the raid, no sign whatsoever was found of any of the much-advertised postal reply coupons.

Prison Gates Swing Open

At a meeting in early August 1920 with his auditor, Edwin L. Pride, Ponzi still kept insisting that he was solvent. In his opinion, there was an organised plot to ruin him, a plot that originated from jealous bankers in Boston and the government.

On their part the auditor and his staff had concluded that Ponzi owed nearly $6 million. The Hanover bank's president, Chmielinski, reported that bank commissioner Allen had decided to close down the Hanover bank because its financial situation was unsound.

Finally, in a meeting on 12 August 1920 with the auditor Pride, bank commissioner Allen, attorney Gallagher and two detectives, Ponzi confessed that he had $7 million in debts and only $3 million in assets. Pride was the first one to find his voice and he pointed out that Ponzi was then $4 million short.

According to Donald Dunn, Ponzi responded with a smile that spread from ear to ear: "Gee, then I guess that I'm not solvent." That said, he turned to the US marshal who had moved to his side and said, "Okay, I'm your prisoner."

Ponzi had shown the people of Boston a spectacular swindling play. Nothing of that sort had been seen before in the US investment world. About 17,000 people had invested quite a few million dollars in total with Ponzi.

Many of the unfortunate investors had continued to put their trust in the man until the bitter end. Or they refused even then to admit their own foolishness. They still regarded Ponzi as their hero.

Investors who turned over their notes to the state – many did not, holding on to the belief that Ponzi somehow would yet make good on his promise of 50 per cent interest – received less than 30 cents for each dollar invested.

In the federal trial in November 1920, Ponzi admitted his guilt and was sentenced to five years in the Plymouth Federal Prison for mail fraud. He was released after three and a half years to attend the trial at the state level in Massachusetts. In this second trial he was sentenced to a further seven to nine years in the Massachusetts State Prison.

Out on bail while the verdict was appealed, Ponzi hurried to Florida in a desperate attempt to raise money for his legal battles. As one of the managers of the Charpon Land Syndicate he joined several other tricksters selling swampland in Columbia county to gullible buyers as "prime Florida property". Part of the land was actually under water. Soon, a Jacksonville court found him guilty of fraud.

Ponzi appealed against the Florida sentence and was again set free on a $1,500 bail. In May 1926 word reached him that the Supreme Judicial Court of Massachusetts had upheld his earlier conviction. He now fled to Texas, with two states on his trail.

In Houston he signed aboard an Italian freighter as a seaman. Unfortunately for him, the ship still docked in New Orleans on its way to Genoa. He was recognised despite a brand new moustache and a shaved head and taken off the ship.

Ponzi was returned to Massachusetts. He started serving his sentence at the state prison at Charleston. Several times a month he was visited by his steadfast wife, Rose, who had secured a job as a secretary and bookkeeper in the famed Coconut Grove nightclub in Boston.

During his years in prison, government-assigned auditors tried to delve into Ponzi's complicated accounts. Their main objective was to assess how much money he had amassed and where it had ended up.

A final bankruptcy report was filed 11 years later, in 1931, after weary officials had tried to piece together the incomplete and muddled records of the Securities Exchange Company. One conclusion was that no money had remained in the hands of Ponzi himself.

Ponzi's First Class Return to Italy

Having expiated his sins by more than 12 years in prison in the US in the period 1920–1934, Ponzi walked out the prison gates a free man in February 1934. His wife Rose was waiting for him outside.

But Ponzi was also, according to Donald Dunn, "welcomed" by a crowd of infuriated investors who had lost plenty of money. And by some immigration officials armed with a deportation warrant sending him back to Italy as an undesirable alien, as he had never bothered to apply for US citizenship.

Ponzi's departure to Italy was reminiscent of a farewell party for a celebrity. At Boston harbour he was escorted by seven uniformed immigration inspectors, several of whom carried his luggage. He was ferried to the liner *S.S. Vulcania* in a government motor launch. Smartly dressed and waving his cap in salute, he stepped aboard the ship as newsreel cameras whirred and flashbulbs exploded around him.

At a press conference held in a luxurious first-class suite on the ship, Ponzi disclosed that his friends (probably happy pyramid winners) had put up $95 on top of the US government's $105 for a third-class ticket so that he could travel first class – but of course, only one way. The government also gave him $500 to buy Italian liras to help him start a new life in his home country.

Having wished President Franklin D. Roosevelt success in his New Deal economic recovery programme, Ponzi's famous last words to journalists were: "I went looking for trouble and I found it."

At noon, the ship steamed out from Boston harbour towards the open sea. The colourful deportee was held in the ship's arrest quarters until the *Vulcania* was three miles out at sea.

Rose Ponzi stayed in Boston and filed for divorce in 1937, on the grounds that her husband was a convicted criminal. From the very start it was evident that Rose had not been mixed up in his illegal activities at all.

In Donald Dunn's interview with her in Florida in the early 1970s, it emerged that Rose had remarried, and with her new husband, lived in a small apartment above a garage. Still working at 70, Rose helped her husband run a concession stand at a dog-racing track.

On the phone, she replied: "Rich?" with great weariness in her voice. "When the police took him away and closed all the bank accounts, I was left with nothing more than his 68-year-old mother to take care of."

Unpublished Memoirs

Carlo Ponzi's arrival in Rome was far less spectacular than his departure from the US. He returned from his fabled Eldorado with almost empty pockets. He finally managed to find work as a movie company bookkeeper, and later got a slightly better job as a construction materials salesman.

His lowly salary of about $100 a week was barely enough to pay his rent for a furnished room in a cheap area in the outskirts of Rome. There he started writing his autobiography, *The Rise of Mr. Ponzi*. In a letter to Rose, he asked her to borrow money from friends in order for him to publish the book.

To finance the publication of his memoirs, Ponzi offered shares in it – 1,000 shares at $20 each. With a straight face he told prospects that he could promise a 100 per cent interest because it was no illusion that 25,000 copies could be sold in New England alone.

When his plan failed, he instructed a friend in the United States to ask a Brooklyn print shop to run off 1,000 copies of the book. But the printer refused to deliver them until the $235 printing bill was paid.

Since it remained unpaid, the whole edition was destroyed. Only one single typed copy of the autobiography has been found in the Library of Congress. According to Dunn, the book is almost unbelievably well written for a self-taught immigrant who, after 15 years in the US, had become a "patriotic cuss".

The memoirs are rich in names, places and figures. The vibrant book bursts with anecdotes and humorous comments on the credulity of fellow men. However, as it was written in Rome in 1937, almost 20 years after the events, there are allegedly wide disparities between his version and newspaper reports.

Destination Rio de Janeiro

One of his closest friends and mentors was his second cousin, Colonel Attilio Biseo, of the Italian air force, commander of the Green Mice Squadron and the personal pilot of Prime Minister Benito Mussolini. Biseo gave the ageing swindler enough cash for him to get drunk occasionally and gamble at penny ante card games in a neighbourhood bar.

Having concluded the book project, Ponzi eventually returned to work as an interpreter for hotels in Venice and Rome. A new career opened up for him in 1939. Leading his squadron, Colonel Biseo flew to Rio de Janeiro to discuss the creation of an airline between Brazil and Italy. Biseo offered his second cousin a job as business manager of the new airline, the LATI. Ponzi promptly accepted the offer and left for Rio by steamer.

He moved to a pleasant two-storey house in the centre of Rio and was happy as a bird, with two servants and a chauffeur at his disposal. His close associates were the Italian ambassador and Colonel Vicenze Coppola, who headed the airline. The twice-monthly flights to Rome became quite popular with businessmen and government officials alike.

The outbreak of World War II in Europe triggered an investigation into the airline's activities. The authorities in Rio concluded that the planes were used to smuggle Brazilian diamonds and strategic materials to the Axis, and carried out a two-way traffic in spies, microfilm and escaped military figures. In December 1941, as the US entered the war after the Japanese attack on Pearl Harbor, the Brazilian Government cut off the supplies of gasoline to LATI. Ponzi was again out of a job.

Evening Tattoo

An eternal optimist, Ponzi tried to sell his story about the LATI affair to various newspapers, but was met with little interest. Using his savings, he bought a small rooming house, but was forced to sell it as the neighbours complained that his roomers were mainly prostitutes.

After that he opened a hot dog stand boasting that he would start a chain of them across the whole country. But after only a few months Ponzi closed the stand and bought a shabby apartment on Copacabana Beach, where he made a precarious living as a teacher of English and French.

He was forced to sell his apartment and move to a rented room in a working-class suburb far from the sea. Still, he earned $300 a month as an interpreter for an Italian import firm.

Ponzi suffered a stroke in 1948 which partly paralysed him. He also went blind in one eye, and was transferred to a charity hospital in Rio de Janeiro.

In hospital Ponzi still managed to grant a farewell interview to an American journalist. He gave a vivid account of the drama that he had offered the Bostonians:

> "Even if they never got anything for it, it was cheap at
> that price. Without malice aforethought I had given them
> the best show that was ever staged in their territory
> since the landing of the Pilgrims. It was easily worth
> fifteen million bucks to watch me put the thing over."

The charmer, adventurer and swindler, who had all his life dreamt about a millionaire's sweet life, died on 18 January 1949, at the age of 66.

RISE AND FALL OF THE WORLD'S MATCH KING, IVAR KREUGER

Eminent construction engineer, the world's match king, financial genius, Europe's takeover magnate, strategic owner of some of Sweden's largest companies and ultimately, after the collapse of his corporate empire, a swindler whose life was extinguished by his own hand in Paris. In brief, that is the colourful life story of Sweden's most celebrated and, in the end, most disgraced corporate tycoon.

Ivar Kreuger was born in the city of Kalmar in Southern Sweden in 1880. The family had originally emigrated to Sweden from Northern Germany in the late 1600s. Ivar Kreuger's father was the industrialist and Russian consul, Ernst Kreuger. Consequently, life as an entrepreneur came naturally to Ivar as a legacy from his father and grandfather.

Kreuger passed the student exam at the unusually young age of 16, having skipped over two annual classes. In the Stockholm Royal Institute of Technology he continued at his frantic pace: in the exceptionally short time span of three years, he passed two different engineering exams, the first one in mechanical engineering, and the other in road and water construction. The 20-year-old double engineer's feat was a new record in the history of the institute.

At its peak in 1930, the Swedish Match Corporation (STAB) headed by Kreuger commanded no less than 75 per cent of the world's match markets. Matches were quite important in those days. Less known abroad is that Kreuger was instrumental in creating and even a major owner in several Swedish world-class companies quoted on the Stockholm Stock Exchange.

Among those were two large forest industry companies, Svenska Cellulosa Aktiebolaget SCA and Stora Kopparbergs Ab, the telephone company L. M. Ericsson, the two mining companies, Boliden and LKAB, and the noted ball bearing producer, SKF.

STAB's successor, Swedish Match, established in 1992, is active internationally and quoted on the Stockholm Stock Exchange. The company has 15,000 employees in the fields of tobacco products and lighting products.

The Engineer's Successful Take-Off

As a young engineer and future world conqueror, Ivar Kreuger left Sweden right after graduation to start a career abroad. At first he earned a living as a real estate agent in the US within Swedish immigrant circles, and after that as a construction engineer.

He made his way to Mexico in 1901 in the company of nine other young engineers to start working in Vera Cruz with a bridge construction company. Unluckily for them, the whole group was cut down by yellow fever. Only Kreuger and another friend survived. Having returned to Sweden to recover, Kreuger reported for military service, but was rejected for medical reasons.

The almost unlimited business prospects in the US made an unforgettable impression on the young Kreuger. The American lifestyle fascinated him and he admired the dynamic entrepreneurial spirit in the US – which was later reflected in his whole attitude towards life.

Having recovered fully from the yellow fever he decided to return to the US, where he became a planning engineer for some skyscraper projects. As an inquisitive and energetic engineer, Kreuger soon mastered American construction techniques and working methods.

In the summer of 1903 new challenges beckoned. Kreuger contacted the technical consulting firm, M.A. Porter, in London, which was engaged in a major hotel complex in South Africa's Johannesburg. Kreuger was hired to supervise the construction of the Carlton hotel.

Once the Carlton project had been completed, it turned out that the construction sector was very quiet. Kreuger decided to establish a restaurant with his life-long Norwegian friend, Anders Jordahl. It was financed with a loan from his father. The restaurant was successful and after some time could be sold at a nice profit.

Kreuger then travelled to Africa and India and studied French in Paris. In 1905 the restless young man returned to the US, this time as chief engineer of a construction company, supervising some large-scale construction projects at the Syracuse University, among other things.

The return to Sweden took place under lucky stars. Kreuger had cooperated closely with the Trussed Concrete Steel Company in Detroit. It had made a pioneering invention in steel reinforced concrete, the so-called Kahn method. Prior to his return to Sweden, Kreuger had secured the right to represent the new technique in Sweden and Germany.

He wrote a comprehensive article about it in the prestigious Swedish technical magazine, *Teknisk Tidskrift*. Steel reinforced concrete had earlier been used only sparsely in Sweden, but from then on its popularity rose rapidly.

In order to cater to the Swedish construction market Kreuger and his new friend, Paul Toll, also a construction engineer, founded a construction company named Kreuger & Toll in 1908. The company took off to a flying start, thanks to the new construction technique.

On its merit list were many large projects, such as the Stockholm Stadium, which served as the main arena for the 1912 Olympic games; the large Nordiska Kompaniet department store; the Holmen paper factory and the foundations of the Stockholm City Hall, as pointed out in banker Lars-Erik Thunholm's book on Kreuger's life.

March Towards the World's Match King Throne

Although his construction company's success story continued, the hyperactive Kreuger turned his eye towards the match industry in 1912 as the family-owned match factory had been hit by some financial setbacks.

An experienced banking friend advised Kreuger to convert it into a limited company, which would facilitate its financing as the shares could be used as collateral for loans.

In almost no time the energetic Kreuger succeeded in merging about 20 small match factories into one large company. He rose to become the new firm's chief executive.

Without losing time Kreuger took the bull by the horns and initiated talks with the owners of Sweden's largest match factory by far. After complicated negotiations he succeeded in creating a new leading company, the Swedish Match Company (STAB).

In the early 1900s matches were needed everywhere in great quantities for fireplaces, stoves, oil lamps and smoking, not to mention candles. In due course, the new company – of course with Kreuger as its CEO – became the world's leading producer of matches. Everywhere in the world, the high-quality Swedish safety matches had an excellent reputation, and 90 per cent of the production was exported.

Gradually Kreuger managed to gain a monopoly, or at least a commanding position, in the markets in Sweden, Finland, Norway and Denmark, as well as in many other European and faraway populous countries.

In the 1920s three quarters of the world's match production was in Kreuger's hands. In Europe his production share exceeded a phenomenal 90 per cent, which under the present European Union competition rules would be completely out of the question.

Money talked. Ivar Kreuger conquered the foreign match markets with the help of money. His brilliant strategy was to offer attractive, sizeable, so-called "friendship loans" to various governments that were in need of more financing – *inter alia* France, Germany, Italy, Poland, Turkey, Greece, Hungary, Yugoslavia, the Baltic countries and Romania – on the condition that STAB was granted a monopoly in their match markets.

As always in the case of monopoly, the end of competition created space for price rises, which of course improved STAB's profitability. But the governments and thereby the tax payers in those countries also benefited from Kreuger's new strategy: on the one hand, they received urgently-needed currency loans on favourable terms, and on the other, each government got its share of the monopoly profits.

Kreuger's strategy was like magic, a win-win proposition. All parties appreciated it, perhaps with the exception of consumers who probably had to pay a higher price for their matches.

Kreuger's Groundbreaking Funding Strategy

These friendship loans and the febrile international takeover pace strained STAB's financial situation, as the aggressive global strategy required a great deal of borrowing by STAB from Swedish banks. Gradually, the ceiling started to come down.

But the resourceful Kreuger succeeded in opening up a new, loaded financing channel. It helped him to break away from the clutches of his own country's smallish banks and their limited lending potential. The name of the new horn of plenty was the United States.

Thanks to Kreuger's superb negotiation skills, Lee Higginson & Co became STAB's leading financier. Higginson was in the top tier among the investment banks in the almost unlimited US capital market.

The investment banks acted as wholesale banks. The largest US companies received most of their financing through these banks, which also managed the portfolio investments of thousands of the wealthiest Americans.

Lee Higginson & Co had already been founded in 1848 and enjoyed respect in wide investor circles because of its professional and conservative management. The five leading US investment banks at the time were J. P. Morgan, Kuhn Loeb, and Speyer in New York, as well as Kidder Peabody and Lee Higginson in Boston. With the help of its nationwide office network,

Higginson's placing power for both securities and straight corporate loans was exceptionally strong.

Kreuger's personality made a great impression on Higginson's top management. For the next ten years the bank acted as the main supplier of Kreuger's international financing.

Thousands of rich American private investors and firms soon bought shares and other securities issued by STAB. This wide-open financing channel considerably reduced Kreuger's dependence on the much smaller Swedish commercial banks, which were already more than overburdened by the financing needs related to Kreuger's continuous corporate buyouts.

In order to make his company better known on the other side of the Atlantic, Kreuger decided to establish a pure holding company in the United States, the International Match Corporation (IMCO). It was not involved in production or marketing, but Kreuger recognised that a US firm (though owned by the parent company) paved the way for American capital into the worldwide match conglomerate.

Kreuger succeeded in attracting several prominent banking and industry personalities onto the IMCO board. Although the board was not a decision-making body, it inspired a lot of confidence in STAB. Kreuger himself, of course, continued to make all the important financial decisions, and he also had sole responsibility for the company's broad strategic and tactical guidelines.

Kreuger's Career Peaking

Kreuger's career as an international industrialist and financial wizard peaked in the spring of 1929. His conglomerate's success story had been spurred by the worldwide economic boom and the huge financial resources that he had been instrumental in mobilising.

STAB's shares were traded on most of the world's important stock exchanges, as one of the very few stocks with a completely international nature.

The economic boom gradually evolved into real euphoria, a belief in everlasting enrichment. It was a little reminiscent of the situation in the world's stock markets in the 1990s and from 2000–2007.

As one of Kreuger's historians, Lars-Erik Thunholm estimated that an almost unbelievable 1.4 billion Swedish crowns (close to 40 billion crowns or €4 billion in today's money) had been issued in stocks, bonds and debentures for the account of STAB, IMCO and Kreuger & Toll.

The gigantic debt burden is illustrated by the fact that the outstanding loan stock of the Swedish banks was about 4 billion crowns in those days. Accordingly, the domestic and foreign debt of Kreuger's match empire was equivalent to one third of the total Swedish bank debt – a tremendous concentration of financial risk within Sweden's banking system.

The Kreuger conglomerate had an incredibly important strategic role in the Swedish economy. Its share of the market value of the Stockholm Stock Exchange was nearly one half. Partly for this reason, the Swedish markets were inundated with Kreuger securities. But in the US, the situation was comfortable, with thousands of investors continuing to buy Kreuger shares and debentures, even at rising prices.

To sum it up, Kreuger had achieved something monumental: his conglomerate owned 250 match-producing companies in 43 countries, it had a monopoly in 25 countries and it produced three quarters of all the world's matches. He had transferred 1.5 billion Swedish crowns in loans to 15 countries. This was a unique achievement in Sweden's industrial history.

The Turnaround

In the spring of 1929, there were already some small signs in the air that the speculative stock market boom was abating. But Kreuger did not slow down or even take a breather. In spite of warnings from his trusted adviser and friend, banker Oscar Rydbeck, Kreuger, in the summer of 1929, continued to hatch aggressive additional borrowing plans to finance new daring business ventures in various countries.

All of a sudden, Black Thursday on the New York Stock Exchange on 24 October 1929 interrupted the speculative bubble of all time. It completely undermined Kreuger's bold financing strategy.

The first victims were a few carefully planned and badly needed loans from the American and European capital markets, for a total of 300 million Swedish crowns. Kreuger launched the loans in the midst of the financial hurricane, and they turned out to be gigantic failures. Despite Kreuger's active support buying, the loans remained largely unsubscribed.

Even in this catastrophic setting Kreuger steadied his nerves. During the disastrous autumn of 1929 he did not hesitate to grant a large loan to the German government to clinch a match monopoly in this important country. STAB's financial pressures were exacerbated by earlier agreements for new loans amounting to $60 million in total to Poland, Turkey, Bolivia, Guatemala, Greece and Lithuania, in which he also hoped to secure a match monopoly.

Despite such dire straits, Kreuger did not recognise or admit that a liquidity crisis was looming. With the benefit of hindsight, we can perhaps recognise that he seemed to have already lost touch with reality. He lived in a different world, in a castle in the air, and his world was full of new attractive business opportunities, according to Thunholm.

When STAB's share price started to totter, Kreuger continued to sacrifice hundreds of millions of Swedish crowns for even more support purchases. Their stabilising effect on the stock turned out to be minimal and the support buying was nearly a complete waste of money.

Birthday Celebration Without A Guest of Honour

Almost all of Sweden celebrated Ivar Kreuger's 50th birthday on 2 March 1930. The newspapers sang his praise in solemn articles, and his home in Villagatan in Stockholm was flooded by telegrams and other congratulations.

But the birthday boy escaped the rumpus and travelled abroad to an unknown destination. Did he perhaps already have a premonition that soon he would not celebrate?

Kreuger's withdrawn nature is illustrated by the following: having learnt that his friends had written birthday memoirs in his honour, Kreuger resolutely prohibited the book's distribution and saw to it that the whole edition was destroyed. Only one copy remains, apparently the one which, according to normal practice, had been sent directly to Kungliga Biblioteket, Sweden's national library.

The Noose Tightens

In April 1931 the conglomerate's financing outlook turned absolutely critical. Most reluctantly, the Skandinaviska Banken, which Kreuger controlled, threw in another 135 million crowns.

The Kreuger empire now owed a record 275 million crowns to Skandinaviska Banken. This represented an exceptional one-third of the bank's total credit stock. Such reckless risk concentration in one single enterprise was not in line with any sound banking practices.

In addition, Sweden's central bank, Riksbanken, agreed after much hesitation to come to the rescue by granting a 20-million crown rediscount limit to Skandinaviska Banken.

In his desperate search for further financing, Kreuger continued to travel in the US. President Herbert Hoover received him in the White

House since he wanted the advice of this globally respected business leader on ways and means of solving the raging economic crisis.

In the autumn of 1931 the always alert Swiss newspapers sounded the alarm. The business publication, *Schweitzerische Handelszeitung*, wrote a critical article about Kreuger's financial dilemma. They were, of course, worried by the collapse in the prices of his shares and debentures.

In an unusually blunt comment, the mighty Crédit Suisse bank branded Kreuger "a very dangerous man".

The Swiss had, as always, a cool and realistic picture of the situation.

Share Price Collapse and Liquidity Squeeze

According to the Affärsvärlden magazine share index, the price of the Kreuger-shares dropped by an astounding 71 per cent in the 12 months up to December 1931. In this fix Kreuger was forced to apply for more assistance from Riksbanken.

His unwelcome loan request was rejected twice, but when the government sympathetically started to exert pressure on the central bank, it relented and granted Kreuger another 40-million-crown loan. But the Riksbanken budged only after it had received Kreuger's shares in the large Boliden mining and metal company as collateral.

Faced with his liquidity squeeze, Kreuger came up with a new idea: he agreed to sell his majority stake in the telephone firm, L. M. Ericsson, to the large American ITT company for $11 million (over $170 million today). However, after the deal, the buyer was shocked to find that some of the information which Kreuger had submitted about L.M. Ericsson's cash position and profit outlook was clearly incorrect.

In particular, ITT was upset that the valuable item, "cash and bank", in the accounts in reality represented only a claim on Kreuger & Toll. Accordingly, ITT's management requested an immediate cancellation of the deal.

When the ITT crisis was at its worst in February–March 1932, the stressed Kreuger suffered a nervous breakdown on this last trip to the US. The doctor diagnosed it as a "brain fag". He recovered quickly and resumed his feverish work schedule since he was about to leave for business talks in Paris. After Paris, he would continue to Berlin to discuss vital additional funding with the legendary Swedish central bank governor Ivar Rooth (who, by the way, served as the IMF's managing director from 1951–1956).

During the visit Kreuger was informed that ITT had secured a departure prohibition order from the passport authorities, preventing him from leaving the US unless he agreed to cancel the ITT agreement and return the full purchase price of $11 million. Alternatively, he could put up an acceptable surety for the repayment.

Having no choice, Kreuger signed the deal cancellation. This took place on 4 March 1932. In the afternoon he stepped aboard the *Ile de France* sailing to Europe.

Last Lies Into the Open

The clock ticked louder and louder. After the pleasant seven-day ocean crossing Kreuger arrived on 11 March at his comfortable apartment in the centre of Paris in Avenue Victor Emmanuel III. He was met by a few of his accounting officers coming from Stockholm.

His subordinates posed some extremely delicate questions which Kreuger alone could answer. They concerned the corporate accounts for 1931, which were to be published quite soon.

The accountants were above all intrigued by the item "Italian State treasury bills" for a counter-value of £25 million (a whopping £1,300 million today). Kreuger had on several occasions referred to them as highly valuable assets. They now wanted to know with what means these securities had been paid, because no corresponding expense item had been detected.

Kreuger answered hesitantly that interest had been paid on these securities and that they were genuine.

At this point Kreuger left for Hotel Meurice to meet his trusty banking friend, Oscar Rydbeck. Even this gentleman brought up the Italian treasury bills and asked if they could not be sold in order to mobilise additional cash. Kreuger countered by saying that he had agreed not to sell them or to pledge them as collateral.

Rydbeck then proposed an alternative solution: sell them to the Italian Government at a discount. This proposal was also answered evasively: Kreuger would then be forced to travel to Italy to negotiate a deal, and such discussions would demand plenty of time.

Rydbeck concluded the sensitive discussion, proposing to meet again the following morning at 11 o'clock at the Hotel du Rhin. The directors of Lee Higginson & Co would also attend the meeting.

After this Kreuger left for his apartment, where he, as far as is known, spent the evening with a Finnish lady friend.

A Shot Echoes Through Paris

The next morning Kreuger received his long-time colleague, STAB's deputy managing director Krister Littorin, in his apartment. Littorin reported that the previous evening the Americans had shown him a cash forecast, which Kreuger himself had given to Lee Higginson. They had requested that Littorin confirm the accuracy of the figures, but he had refused to do so because quite evidently they were wrong.

When Littorin asked for Kreuger's opinion, he only shrugged his shoulders and said that submitting the cash forecast to them had been a bad idea right from the beginning.

The worried Littorin concluded that Kreuger had deliberately passed a fabricated forecast to his American banking friends. He tried to comfort his cherished boss with the words: "You may have done whatsoever, said whatsoever or written whatsoever, remember that only friends stand by your side, and we wish you nothing but the best and want to help in straightening out everything." Finally he reminded Kreuger about the meeting at 11 o'clock and left the apartment.

At the Hotel du Rhin the Swedes and Americans waited patiently, but time passed and no Kreuger was to be seen. Rydbeck tried to call him several times without success, and finally he suggested that somebody go and check if Kreuger was still in his apartment. Littorin left at a little past 1 o'clock, accompanied by the secretary, Karin Bökman.

When the housekeeper, Ms. Barrault, opened the door, they were told that Kreuger was sound asleep – as Ms. Barrault had seen when she had peeped into the room. Littorin knocked on the door, opened it and entered. The anxious women were waiting outside when they suddenly heard Littorin's terrified voice: "*Il ne dort pas, il est mort!*" (He's not asleep, he is dead!).

Kreuger was lying on his bed fully dressed, except that his suit jacket and vest were unbuttoned. Blood had seeped onto his shirt, over his heart. The pistol was lying on the bed on the right-hand-side of the body, at his feet. On the desk were a few letters. Somewhat surprisingly, he had written to Littorin in English:

> "I have made such a mess of things that I believe this
> to be the most satisfactory solution for everybody
> concerned – Goodbye now and thanks. I. K."

Weapons were nothing new to Kreuger. During his school years he had practised shooting and had become quite an accomplished marksman. He had bought the heavy 9-mm calibre pistol from an arms dealer near his apartment the evening before his suicide.

On the basis of the motives, the position of the body, the farewell letters and the pistol purchase, the French police investigations concluded that it was suicide. But interestingly enough, certain people, including Kreuger's brother, Torsten Kreuger, using more or less convincing arguments, concluded that Kreuger was murdered by his enemies.

His balsamated body was sent in a sealed coffin by train from the Gare du Nord station to Stockholm, where it arrived on 19 March 1932. The French seal was opened in the presence of the relatives and the coffin was taken to the Gustaf Vasa church in preparation for the funeral service to be held on 22 March.

After a short funeral ceremony, attended only by family members and Littorin, the coffin was taken to the Norra Kyrkogården's crematorium. Thousands of people watched the funeral cortege in silence.

The suicide made headline news in the leading newspapers of the Western world. The general conclusion was that Kreuger collapsed as a result of the worldwide economic crash and the liquidity crisis. The conservative daily, *Svenska Dagbladet*, concluded that: "The bullet that extinguished Ivar Kreuger's life did not crush his great achievements."

The economic magazine, *Affärsvärlden*, emphasised that "Kreuger was a brave speculator, but he built his work on foundations which would have been safe in less exceptional circumstances."

The most influential economist of the 20th century, John Maynard Keynes, concluded in his commemorative speech in a *BBC* radio broadcast that: "Here was a man of perhaps the greatest constructive business intelligence of his age…"

Painful Investigations and the Fatal Forgery

The estate inventory was started without delay. The report by the accounting firm, Price Waterhouse, unearthed many shocking facts. It revealed that Ivar Kreuger had manipulated and even falsified STAB's accounts. The accounts and the financial benchmarks had been significantly embellished. Some fictive items had even been used to magnify the 1930 profits.

Ivar Kreuger's name, however, came into a completely new light when it was detected that the much discussed Italian Government treasury bills, which appeared as important corporate assets in the accounts, were actually forged.

Price Waterhouse and, before them, some others, had started to suspect forgery because there was no trace in either the company's books or in Kreuger's correspondence that the huge purchase price of £25 million had actually been paid to the Italian Government.

In reality, Kreuger himself had asked the Börtzell printing house in Stockholm to print these securities. He had personally provided a model copy to the chief printer. Having received the "bonds", Kreuger had forged Italian Finance Minister Mosconi's signature on them in a clumsy manner.

To certify the assumed forgery, a justice of the Swedish Supreme Court, Johannes Hellner, was sent to Rome. The Swedish ambassador organised a meeting with Prime Minister Benito Mussolini. Hellner showed Mussolini the Italian treasury bill found among Kreuger's documents.

When Mussolini saw Mosconi's signature he immediately exclaimed that it was a fake. The prime minister even produced a document that showed the true signature. Mussolini acknowledged that his government had discussed a monopoly agreement with Kreuger, but the negotiations had broken down in the autumn of 1929.

At one go, the shameful forgery of foreign government securities completely destroyed the good reputation of Sweden's most revered industrialist ever. The great Kreuger's downfall suddenly turned into the treacherous Kreuger's swindle!

The revelations led to an almost outrageous witch-hunt in Sweden. In April–May 1932 the Swedish police interrogated a large number of people and arrested several suspects. Ultimately, heavy charges were brought against several directors and top managers of the conglomerate.

Over half a dozen individuals, including two board members, received jail sentences and astronomical damage claims. Some of the sentences could well be questioned because it was impossible to prove that those convicted had indeed acted dishonestly or even had any reason to suspect that their esteemed Kreuger had anything illegal in mind.

The attitude of the judges was clearly influenced by the public outcry, even mass psychosis. People demanded and got several scapegoats – although well informed sources knew full well that Kreuger alone had been responsible for all important corporate decisions.

The Bankruptcy Estate

Bankruptcy was inevitable. The trustees estimated that the capital deficit was 271 million crowns, and because the conglomerate's own capital had been 878 million crowns, the capital destruction ran to roughly 1,150 million crowns (about 31 billion crowns, or €3.4 billion in today's money).

A large part of the capital destruction estimates was, however, due to the fact that the trustees had cleaned out some fictitious or twice-recorded items from the balance sheet for 1930. In the manipulated accounts, some valuable real estate had, for instance, been booked as assets of the Banque de Suède et de Paris, but at the same time, also as assets of the parent company, Kreuger & Toll. Part of the capital deficit was also due to the decline in the prices of the conglomerate's holdings of stocks and bonds in the wake of the global economic crisis.

Kreuger's private estate was deep in debt, by an amazing 1,170 million crowns. Compared with that, its assets were quite small, merely 98 million. The deficit exceeded one billion crowns.

These huge debts were mainly due to the senseless last-minute support purchases of STAB shares, and, perhaps to a lesser extent, to bribes paid to sundry ministers and political parties abroad in order to speed up monopoly negotiations.

The trustees were able to close the books only after nine years of work. On the basis of the remaining assets in the bankrupt estate, the non-preferred creditors received an indemnity of 42 per cent of their claims. The owners of participating debentures were left without any compensation whatsoever. The final result was nevertheless fairly decent and clearly exceeded the original expectations.

Although the valuation of Kreuger's investment portfolio in shares and bonds had dropped considerably, it would have turned out to be quite valuable in the longer run, as it comprised shares in, for instance, STAB, L. M. Ericsson, Svenska Cellulosa Ab and Boliden. Later assessments suggest that thousands of individuals faced bankruptcy as a result of the hasty, even panicky, selling of Kreuger shares.

As a matter of fact, STAB survived the crash, in spite of its heavy debts. It was still profitable. The match empire, which was above all Kreuger's life's work, remained in place for the future.

Kreuger's American Investment Bank Fails

In the American financial sector it turned out to be a catastrophe that one single top-tier investment bank, Lee Higginson & Co, had all alone catered to Kreuger's uninhibited overseas financing needs. Higginson's and its owners' own losses rose to $8 million, but above all the company would bitterly regret that it had allowed Kreuger to deceive it.

As the sole issuer of Kreuger securities, Higginson was instantly blamed for misleading its portfolio investing clients. The US senate's hearings concluded that the firm had not observed normal prudential principles in recommending the purchase of these securities.

Higginson was accused of causing serious losses to thousands of wealthy Americans who had bought Kreuger securities in good faith. Their total investments rose to the enormous sum of $250 million (almost $4 billion today). Higginson was particularly blamed for never requesting (or getting) an independent audit report for the Kreuger conglomerate.

Kreuger's collapse was a mortal blow for Lee Higginson. Its most important trump card had been its solid reputation as a prudent, professionally managed and trustworthy company. This good reputation was now completely destroyed.

The firm had to be liquidated because nobody would entrust money to it anymore. The ruin of Kreuger's empire also swept with it the American holding company, IMCO.

Sweden's Prime Minister Fired

Kreuger's downfall also sealed the fate of Sweden's Prime Minister C. G. Ekman. Having detected some mysterious notes in Kreuger's diaries, the bankruptcy trustees started to suspect that on a couple of occasions a large sum of money had been paid to the prime minister.

This money paid to Ekman was immediately connected to his strong backing of the crisis financing desperately sought by Kreuger before the crash. Besides, the sum involved was significant, 100,000 crowns (about SEK 2.8 million or €300,000 today).

The prime minister at first denied the whole thing. However, after he was confronted with written evidence, he regained his memory and reluctantly admitted that a certain sum had actually been paid to his Liberal party.

As the party did not have any detailed records regarding these funds and their use, it was concluded that in all likelihood part of the money had remained in Ekman's pockets.

Ekman returned the full sum to Kreuger's estate, but that was too late.

He was forced to resign as prime minister, after which he was a politically dead man.

The Winning Wallenbergs

There were also winners. The prominent Wallenberg family's bank, Enskilda Banken, was now rewarded for its cautious attitude towards lending money to the Kreuger conglomerate. The bank's strong liquidity position was partly due to that, according to Lars-Erik Thunholm.

On the strength of their ample financial resources, the Wallenberg group could, after the events, buy a great deal of shares cheaply in the most valuable Kreuger industries, such as L. M. Ericsson, SKF and Grängesberg.

Ivar Kreuger's crash strengthened the Wallenbergs' economic clout in another way as well: because his shares in Skandinaviska Banken had acted as collateral for some loans to him from Enskilda Banken, the Wallenberg bank became at a go the most important shareholder in their competitor, Skandinaviska Banken.

Kreuger's Mystery

How was it possible that an intelligent, competent, serious and globally respected industrialist and financial expert such as Ivar Kreuger could degrade himself by using such dishonest practices? How could he falsify accounts *en masse* and even resort to serious fraud? What did he really think, and how could he imagine that he would be able to get away with it all?

How was he able to fool not only his closest collaborators, but the whole Swedish and international financial establishment, financial analysts, the Western world's stock exchanges and a lot of rich investors? These questions posed by Thunholm deserve some reflection.

During his early career as the dynamic leader of the flourishing construction company, nothing questionable was reported regarding his business practices or accounting principles. Only after the world's economic wheels partly stopped turning in the wake of the economic depression starting in 1929 did he fall into temptation, embellish the accounts and even end up using fraudulent methods.

Window dressing of corporate accounts was nothing completely unique at the time. That was occasionally also used in business circles elsewhere.

Even as the worldwide financial crisis took its toll in 1929–1931, Kreuger could muddle along with the help of almost reckless new borrowing. He also had the kind support of the Swedish central bank and the government.

But after he started to forge Italian state securities, he descended to the level of serious fraud. Kreuger may have imagined that he would still gain a monopoly in Italy, and that he could perhaps benefit from the forged treasury bills as company "assets". In his confused mind, that might have balanced the situation.

Kreuger's skill in covering his tracks was almost unbelievable. That was partly due to his exceptional confidence-inspiring personality, which explained the almost slavish loyalty of his colleagues. He captivated everybody with his charisma.

As one ponders the Kreuger mystery, one should keep in mind that the world has seen great swindlers both before and after him, as shown in this book. In ancient Rome the philosopher, Petronius, summed it up in one sentence: "*Mundus vult decipi, ergo decipiatur*" (The world wants to be deceived, so let it be deceived). Even Martin Luther used the saying "*Mundus vult decipi*".

As he was the son of a small country who entered the world economic stage and triumphed, using practically only his own bare hands, all suspicions disappeared. He became Sweden's pride, and everybody competed for his favour.

Even in December 1931, only three months before his suicide in Paris, Svenska Handelsbanken answered the French Paribas bank's credit information request as follows: "*Considerée absolument bonne pour ses engagements*", which may be translated to "Absolutely good credit rating".

Kreuger also possessed other outstanding personal qualities: he was tactful, dependable and secretive. He also expected the same from his subordinates. When the journalist, Isaac Marcosson, of the *Saturday Evening Post* wondered about the secret of his success, Kreuger replied: "Discretion, more discretion and even more discretion."

He evidently thought that discretion in the extreme was necessary in the delicate monopoly negotiations in which prominent politicians from many countries were involved.

Cold Character and Career Motives

The exceptionally secretive Ivar Kreuger is still an enigma, a mystery, although about 70 books have been written about his life, including Thunholm's comprehensive book.

Kreuger was completely absorbed in his work. He had no normal private life or confidants. He did not keep any extensive diary nor write any notes, and did not engage in any personal correspondence highlighting his inner thoughts. But all and everybody who met him admired his phenomenal memory.

He was no friend of the pleasures of the table, and he used alcohol only moderately. He did not care about wines, perhaps with the exception of good champagne.

After a good meal he could enjoy a glass of fine cognac, but on weekdays he did not normally drink anything else other than mineral water. He smoked cigarettes, but in moderation. Cigars he never smoked.

The leader of the worldwide conglomerate had a heavy travel schedule.

Kreuger was one of the first business tycoons in Sweden to use private planes on business trips within Europe. He normally carried his own suitcase.

Because he detested staying in hotels, Kreuger had his own apartments in Paris, Berlin, New York and Warsaw. Their furnishings did not reflect any particular personal taste. In all of the locations he employed a housekeeper, but no other servants.

Amusements, sports or other forms of entertainment had no place in Kreuger's hectic life. He owned a few holiday villas in the Swedish archipelago, but rarely visited them. But he was in excellent health, despite his pressing workload and lack of recreation.

Ivar Kreuger was always in full control of himself and obviously had steely nerves – with the exception of the one-day nervous breakdown during his last trip to New York in 1932. He never showed any signs of nervousness in business situations, not even in the hour before his suicide. Many people considered him insensitive: no close friends, no hobbies, no openness.

The same emotional frigidity was sensed in his relations with women. He never married or established a family. On the other hand it was rumoured that he was a real womaniser, "with a girl in all ports".

This proved that he enjoyed the relaxing company of women – nothing more. Even his last evening he spent in the company of a woman.

What then were Kreuger's motives? It wasn't money, to say the least, as Kreuger hardly seemed interested in personal wealth. Fame? Hardly that, as he detested publicity and felt awkward in the face of public displays of appreciation. He never sought those, says Thunholm.

What about power? Hardly even power as an absolute value. As an unassuming and discreet person, he was no typical aspirant to power. Power in itself was no goal for him and did not give him satisfaction.

But power as an instrument certainly attracted him. It helped him achieve the many ambitious targets that he put up for himself in life. Therefore his mode of operation was surely autocratic, although he never acted despotically or ruthlessly towards his colleagues.

Ivar Kreuger had only one great vision: to establish a worldwide industrial empire. He sought to achieve this goal through merciless hard work. This all-embracing goal filled his heart and suppressed everything else – and it finally propelled him to ruin, death and disgrace.

PLAYBOY CORNFELD'S
BILLION-DOLLAR STING

The New York Times' obituary in 1995 characterised Bernard Cornfeld as "one of the most flamboyant and controversial figures ever to stride through the American mutual fund industry". He was a true *enfant terrible* of the world of finance.

Bernard Cornfeld's father was a Romanian-Jewish actor, and his mother came from a Russian-Jewish family. Bernard was born in 1927 in Turkey, but the family immigrated to the United States and settled in Brooklyn, New York, when he was four years old.

The father died a couple of years later and after school the young Bernard had to work in a fruit shop and as a messenger boy. He showed a natural talent as a salesman, despite his stammering.

During World War II Cornfeld served in the US Maritime Service, which trained crew and naval officers for the merchant navy. After the war he studied at Brooklyn College in New York and graduated in psychology. In addition, he got a Master's degree from the prestigious Columbia University.

Somewhat surprisingly, Cornfeld started his professional life as a social worker among the poor, in line with his early socialist leaning. But fairly soon he moved to a new career in a firm selling investment fund shares to select investors.

In his new job Cornfeld recognised that the spectrum of services provided by the investment firms could be expanded and also marketed to the public at large – and thereby, so he imagined, the common man could also get rich. He called it "people's capitalism".

Some readers may still remember the illustrious International Overseas Services (IOS) investment fund in the 1960s, and its sad fate. It was one of the first major investment scandals after the war, pictured in detail in the book, *Do You Sincerely Want to Be Rich?*

Bernard Cornfeld's International Overseas Services was a huge fund specialising in investments and portfolio management. Its services were made attractive also because it offered tax shelters to its international clients.

Cornfeld's playing field was his numerous investment funds. The players were a far-flung organisation that included a vast and intensely loyal sales force powered by generous bonuses. The targets were the savings of people living anywhere in the world.

Thousands of investors in Cornfeld's empire lost billions of dollars altogether in today's money – while Cornfeld himself succeeded in escaping from his scam without any extended jail sentence.

Booming Investment Fund

Cornfeld moved from New York to Paris in 1955. He started out selling investments primarily in the Dreyfus Fund, which in those days was a small, less than $2-million fund. Bernard Cornfeld and Jack Dreyfus were close business partners, and Cornfeld bought a ten per cent ownership stake in the fund.

After Cornfeld's own marketing machinery got into full swing, he helped to expand the Dreyfus Fund by channelling several hundred million dollars of investments into its claws. Success was guaranteed by the superior investment instincts of Jack Dreyfus and Cornfeld's brilliant marketing skills and efficient advertising campaigns. Their main theme was a big lion sneaking along Broadway. The investment returns of the Dreyfus Fund regularly surpassed the profits of other similar funds.

Towards the late 1950s, Cornfeld had already accumulated enough money to establish his own fund. The goal of this Overseas Investors Services was, to put it a bit naively, to become the "most important economic force of the free world".

Cornfeld's background in the US Maritime Service was useful, as he could naturally focus his energy on easy targets: at the outset his firm marketed investment funds to hundreds of thousands of US military personnel stationed in Europe and elsewhere, and other expatriates. With the help of his offshore investment firms located in various tax havens these clients could generally circumvent US, European and other taxes. The tax incentive made these investments very popular.

Cornfeld eventually recruited about 25,000 enterprising salesmen. The task of these so-called economic advisers was to rake in the savings of as many people as possible located anywhere in the world. The incoming money was thereafter placed into companies and funds owned by the IOS.

The best salesmen working on bonuses became millionaires as they extracted hefty commission incomes from their clients. They were the cream of the crop.

Cornfeld's action plan was to establish many different types of funds in tax havens. In addition to minimising their taxes, the investors could avoid any other legal constraints put up by their home countries. His offshore firms also included, besides numerous funds, banks, insurance companies, real estate firms and so on. Cornfeld even owned a secretive Swiss bank. The slogan was: "The complete financial service of IOS."

Altogether Cornfeld founded 18 self-owned investment funds, whose investment products and services were sold with great success through door-to-door campaigns to hundreds of thousands of clients. They mostly invested small and medium-size sums, especially in Europe and, most importantly, in Germany. Cornfeld and his salesmen continuously trumpeted the line – with an endearing smile on their faces – "Do You Sincerely Want To Be Rich?"

Cornfeld's Brainwave

Cornfeld's ingenious brainwave was his own 'fund of funds', established in 1962. The fund of funds idea took off like a rocket. No wonder it was and still is copied widely in the investment world.

Its basic idea was the following: in the past, investments had been marketed rationally by emphasising that in the complicated stock and other markets, a common investor needed the advice of an expert as he was seeking to invest his money profitably.

His trailblazing idea went much further: a common investor needed professionals to choose the professionals who allocated their investments into those funds whose value would rise fastest.

Cornfeld's clients were thrilled by the thought that on the volatile global investments markets, the fund of funds balanced their risks with the aid of numerous professionals, especially in the bumpy market environment of the 1960s.

There was also an ulterior and selfish motive behind the fund of funds. Cornfeld turned his firm's investment strategy on its head. The new fund of funds refrained from investing money, as before, into various outside investments funds, but directed their investments mainly into its own individual funds completely managed by the IOS.

As a result, the investors' capital, profits and fees did not leak out into external funds owned by outsiders. Everything was channelled into IOS's own lair. In practice IOS acted as a money gathering centralised fund, into which the millions and eventually billions of dollars flowed and were later placed into its own sub-funds or other purposes favoured by them.

Investors Fleeced

Cornfeld fleeced his clients through multiple commissions and fees. Firstly, commissions on the initial capital investment into the IOS, secondly, commissions for the placement of money into its subsidiary funds, and finally, annual portfolio management fees.

The fee load was simply outrageous. It has been estimated that at least for smaller investments of $3,000, the front-end fees for opening and adding to the account could even consume some 18 per cent of the initial investment value. As if this were not enough, annual running advisory fees, commissions and portfolio management fees were added.

Share prices really had to rise quite sharply before these small investments started to become more profitable than a pedestrian bank deposit anywhere else, because after the deduction of the commissions and fees, the small investor's initial $3,000 eroded down to a meagre $2,460 to be invested in the stock markets.

To cap it all, the clients were fleeced through touted life insurance policies in the offshore insurance company owned by the IOS. Further earnings were generated through the use of IOS's own banks.

During the 1960s IOS managed to amass in investments the almost unbelievable sum of $2.5 billion, which in today's terms would equal almost $15 billion. At its peak IOS had 750,000 clients in 110 countries. Cornfeld's private wealth climbed to more than $100 million (over $600 million today).

Many of Cornfeld's business practices skirted close enough to the edges of federal regulation laws to attract the attention of the SEC. It initiated a close scrutiny of the legality of Cornfeld's operations, and in 1965, accused Cornfeld and his company of violating US securities laws.

After two years of deliberations the IOS came to an agreement with the SEC: its American operations had either to be wound up or sold. As regards Cornfeld's fund of funds, it agreed to buy no more than three per cent of any American mutual fund. That was the federally imposed maximum limit.

The IOS also used other dubious practices. The investors' capital, which was supposed to be held in the IOS for the clients' accounts, was actually "borrowed" to finance IOS's own business operations, or that of its directors and sales agents. IOS also exaggerated the performance of its largest investment fund and hauled in additional hundreds of millions of dollars in investments on the strength of this rosy picture, overestimating its 1969 profits.

The directors and certain top-level staff borrowed so much cash from the company that they almost bankrupted the IOS, thereby hurting the interests of thousands of clients.

The IOS Empire Collapses

No happiness is eternal. When the Dow Jones and many of the world's other stock market indices dropped in two waves towards the late 1960s, it was impossible for the IOS to pay out the promised guaranteed dividends.

At first the management started drawing on the capital – in other words, Cornfeld's fund turned into a type of pyramid scheme, where the existing investors' profits were paid out using new investors' capital. IOS was eating up its capital.

In the second sharp slide at the end of the 1960s, many investors panicked and sold their investment shares. As a result, the IOS share price dropped further, from $18 to $12 per share in the spring of 1970.

The Geneva-based IOS empire had actually been in trouble for some time. While Cornfeld pursued his personal interests – mainly wine, women and gossip column coverage, according to Arthur Herzog – IOS had slipped into disarray. The parent company was losing money, and many of its mutual funds had suffered in a steep stock market decline.

In an effort to remedy the situation, Cornfeld put up an investment pool together with some investors. However, they lost loads of money as the share collapsed to only $2. Even the staff of the IOS and the portfolio managers sold out.

Afterwards Cornfeld blamed some German banks for the crash,

claiming that they had accelerated it by shorting, selling stock futures in the belief that the shares could be bought back later at a lower price (which of course turned out to be very true).

Before the swan song of the IOS, the notorious corporate raider, Robert Vesco (see next chapter), having also run into financial distress, turned to Cornfeld and offered his "help". Vesco was eventually able to get away with more than $200 million of IOS money as he was fighting to save his own International Controls Corporation. When discovered by the SEC, Vesco fled to the Bahamas.

Bernard Cornfeld did everything in his might to save his shattered empire. But he was kicked out from the IOS board in May 1970. The whole IOS group fell to pieces the following year, bringing down with it a few small American and European banks. Till the end of his life, Cornfeld blamed exiled fraudster Vesco for the collapse.

In 1973, three hundred IOS employees charged Cornfeld with defrauding them by selling them stocks in a faltering company. The lawsuit resulted in an 11-month jail sentence for Cornfeld in Switzerland. The final trial took place only in 1979. It lasted three weeks, after which Cornfeld was acquitted. Civil lawsuits recovered some money for fund investors.

Cornfeld's Sweet Lifestyle Continues in Hollywood

Bernard Cornfeld always enjoyed the sweet life. In his days of glory he owned a villa in Geneva, a 13th-century chateau in France, a house in London's posh Belgravia, a palace-like mansion in Hollywood and a permanent suite in a New York hotel. In his heyday he also had several airplanes.

In a newspaper interview Cornfeld bragged about his luxurious life: "I had mansions all over the world, I threw extravagant parties. And I lived with ten or twelve girls at a time."

In the autumn of his life Cornfeld moved to Los Angeles and bought the imposing Grayhall Mansion in Beverly Hills. It had been built in 1909 and was for some time home of the legendary silent film hero, Douglas Fairbanks.

In Los Angeles Cornfeld socialised with the cream of Hollywood personalities. In an effort to tone down his hectic life, Cornfeld married a model, Loraine, even if he from time to time philosophised that "polygamy is considerably simpler than monogamy and a lot more fun".

The millionaire, who during most of his colourful life had lived lavishly, was occasionally stingy in private. In 1976 a Californian court found Cornfeld guilty of fraud for using an electronic device to bypass the billing process for long-distance telephone calls. He was sentenced to three months in prison.

During his last years Bernard Cornfeld turned into a health food freak, renounced red meat and seldom drank alcohol.

The *enfant terrible* suffered a stroke and died of cerebral aneurysm in London in February 1995. He reached the age of 67. Because the marriage with Loraine had ended up in divorce, his daughter Jessica Cornfeld inherited what was left of his shattered empire. She published an article in the British conservative newspaper, *The Mail on Sunday*, in June 2003 entitled "My Father, the Playboy Who Could Never Get Enough Lovers".

ROBERT VESCO,
AMERICA'S MOST
FAMOUS RASCAL

Millionaire Through Hostile Takeovers at Age 30

Robert Vesco was a disreputable American financier who engaged in many high-stake investments and seedy credit dealings, until he fled the country when accused by the SEC of securities fraud. In 1986, *Fortune* magazine nicknamed him "America's most famous rascal".

Vesco was born in Detroit, Michigan, in 1935. The son of an American-Italian Detroit autoworker at Chrysler, he dropped out of Cass Technical High School in his early twenties. After that he went to work in an investment firm.

In the next stage he struck out independently and started matching buyers and sellers in the aluminium market. Later he recalled having had three goals in life: "To get the hell out of Detroit, be president of a corporation and become a millionaire". He was able to buy the International Controls Corporation (ICC) at the young age of 30, and soon became the millionaire he had been dreaming about.

He rode the Wall Street boom in the 1960s, exploiting heavy borrowing and creative accounting. Through aggressive expansions and debt-financed hostile takeovers of other businesses, ICC grew quickly. He also used ICC shares to buy bigger companies. By 1968 Vesco already owned an airline and several manufacturing plants. He also held shares totalling $50 million.

ICC director Larry Richardson was quoted as saying: "He could talk you right out of your socks or blast you out of them, or you could find somebody else owned your socks."

Vesco was a notorious swindler throughout his life. He even attempted to buy an island called Barbuda from Antigua with a view to establishing it as a sovereign state. From there he could have pursued his shady activities freely, and hid safely, without any danger of being extradited to the United States for trials.

Vesco's Hostile Bid for IOS

In a bid to "help" Bernard Cornfeld in his fight to save International Overseas Services in 1970, Vesco launched a takeover bid for the company, as mentioned in the previous chapter. The investment fund, IOS, had at the time holdings of $1.5 billion. As Cornfeld had run into trouble with the SEC and his firm was in financial distress, no "white knight" was willing to get involved in the battle between Cornfeld and Vesco.

Vesco saw his chance and began a protracted battle to assume control of the company, opposed by Cornfeld and others. Exploiting the panicking directors' false belief that IOS needed cash, Vesco negotiated a "rescue" package loan of just $5 million, which he had borrowed himself.

On this basis, he was elected to the IOS board of directors in September 1970. Cornfeld was bought out in January 1971 for another borrowed $5.5 million. Very soon a great deal of IOS assets started to be moved to companies and banks controlled by Vesco.

The battle turned nasty. Cornfeld was thrown in jail in Switzerland and Vesco was accused of looting the company of hundreds of millions of dollars.

Many prominent figures in global business, finance and royalty were tied to the mess, receiving money from one party or the other for support. Vesco was accused of parking funds belonging to IOS investors in various dummy corporations. One of them had an Amsterdam address and it was later linked to Prince Bernhard of the Netherlands.

Flight to the Caribbean

As Vesco was sued in the US for looting the IOS and for securities fraud, he fled to the Caribbean area and, according to *The New York Times,* took with him about $220 million in assets (about $1.1 billion today). He lived the good life in the Bahamas and especially in Costa Rica. There he donated $2.1 million to the Sociedad Agricola Industrial San Cristobal, S.A., founded by President José Figueres.

Vesco lived ostentatiously under Figueres' wing for six years. He had a palatial estate in San José, a vast ranch in the hinterlands, a fleet of vehicles and several armed guards, according to Arthur Herzog.

To thank Vesco, Figueres helped to pass a law guaranteeing that Vesco could not be extradited to the United States. Figueres' constitutional term ended in 1974. Vesco remained in Costa Rica until 1978, when President Rodrigo Carazo repealed what was popularly referred to as the "Vesco Law". He had indeed overstayed his welcome.

Vesco returned to the Bahamas in 1978. After doing business with his neighbour, Colombian drug cartel kingpin Carlos Lehder, he was forced to leave in 1981.

The leftist Sandinistas gave Vesco shelter in Nicaragua in 1982. They also smoothed his later passage to Cuba.

For a change, Vesco also lived temporarily in Antigua. He was well received as the country hoped that he would donate money for various local development projects.

Vesco had rich tastes – homes, yachts, cars and planes. He partied lavishly, chain-smoked and talked big. Only the US president also had a private Boeing 707, but Air Force One did not, unlike the "Silver Phyllis", have a disco and a sauna. Norma Levy, a call girl, once recounted how Vesco and a bevy of hookers partied in the sky while the Boeing 707 circled the skies over Europe.

The Undisputed King of Fugitive Financiers

On the strength of the great wealth that Vesco had amassed, he figured several times in *Forbes* magazine's list of the 400 richest Americans. His occupation was quoted as "thief". A *Slate* magazine article labelled Vesco as "the Undisputed King of Fugitive Financiers".

Vesco's name was also connected with President Richard Nixon. Shortly before fleeing to the Caribbean and hoping to shut off the SEC investigation into his activities, Vesco routed substantial contributions to Richard Nixon through his nephew, Donald A. Nixon.

The hyperactive Vesco was also investigated for an alleged secret $200,000 contribution made to the 1972 campaign to re-elect Nixon. As counsel to the International Controls Corporation, New Jersey lawyer Harry L. Sears reportedly delivered the contribution to Maurice Stans, finance chairman for the Committee to Re-Elect the President.

Vesco had apparently hoped that Attorney General John N. Mitchell would intercede on his behalf with SEC chairman Willian J. Casey. While Vesco fled the country, Stans, Mitchell and Sears were indicted for obstruction of justice, but the charges against all three were later dismissed.

Cuba Libre First, Then Castro's Jail

In his everlasting fight to avoid extradition to the US, Vesco moved to Cuba in 1982. He was allowed in on "humanitarian" grounds. He had also organised some deals to break US sanctions. Besides, Cuba was a country which could provide him with treatment for his painful urinary tract infection.

The Cuban authorities accepted Vesco and agreed not to extradite him to the US on the condition that he would not get involved in any financial deals. He lived with a Cuban woman, Lidia Alfonsa Llauger.

However, the seasoned criminal could not stay away from profitable rackets. In 1989, Vesco was indicted on drug smuggling charges, but was acquitted.

In the 1990s, Vesco became involved once again with Donald A. Nixon as Nixon visited Cuba seeking to partner the government in conducting clinical trials on a substance he claimed would boost immunity, called trixolan or TX. Vesco introduced Nixon to Fidel Castro and his brother, Raul Castro, and the Cuban Government agreed to provide laboratory facilities and doctors to conduct the trials.

The results from the studies were supposedly positive, but eventually TX turned out to be a bogus wonderdrug. In May 1995, Vesco reportedly tried to defraud Nixon and Raul Castro. The Cuban authorities seized control of the project and arrested a haggard and grey Vesco and his common law wife, Llauger. Donald Nixon was detained for questioning, but was released 30 days later.

At the time of Vesco's arrest, the Cuban Foreign Ministry stated that he had been taken into custody "under suspicion of being a provocateur and an agent of foreign special services" – that is, intelligence agencies. He was formally charged with "fraud and illicit economic activity" and "acts prejudicial to the economic plans and contracts of the state".

In 1996, the government sentenced Vesco to 13 years in dreary Cuban jail on charges stemming from the scandal. He was scheduled for release in 2009, when he would have turned 74.

However, Vesco reportedly died of lung cancer in November 2007 and was buried at Colon Cemetery in Havana. His Cuban wife, Lidia, had been convicted on lesser charges and was released from prison in 2005. He was survived by his estranged wife Pat and five children.

Stanley Gaze, one of Vesco's helpers in the IOS, provided a fitting epitaph of Vesco. In his less than flattering characterisation, he described him as

"a sonofabitch who hurt, denigrated or corrupted everyone he had contact with".

ENRON'S MONUMENTAL
CORPORATE SCANDAL

14

The Most Important Corporate Scandal of Our Lifetime

According to the securities law historian, Professor Joel S. Seligman, the Enron case

> "... was the most important corporate scandal of our lifetimes. It was one of the immediate causes of the... most consequential reorientation of corporate behavior in living memory".

The story of Enron's chairman and CEO, Kenneth Lay, is surely amazing: rising from a poor Baptist family to the top of one of the world's largest energy companies, which went bankrupt in 2001 in a tangled web of frauds.

The Enron scandal also caused the demise of the renowned accounting and consulting firm, Arthur Andersen, whose worldwide network employed over 110,000 people.

Kenneth Lay was born in 1942. He studied economics at the University of Missouri and got his PhD in economics from the University of Houston in Texas in 1970.

After graduation he was employed by Exxon before he became a federal energy regulator. In the next stage of his career, he rose to undersecretary in the Department of the Interior.

He returned to the business world as an executive of Florida Gas. By the time energy was deregulated in the 1980s, Lay was already an established energy company executive. He took advantage of the new liberal climate when the Omaha-based Internorth bought his company, Houston Natural Gas, and changed the name to Enron. The much larger, better capitalised and more diversified Internorth was then used to promote his transformation of Enron.

The resourceful Lay was appointed head of Enron in 1986. Under his command the huge company embarked on an entirely new strategy, establishing numerous subsidiaries in tax havens. They were ruthlessly exploited in the company's intricate window-dressing of its accounts, and also to circumvent American taxation. The subsidiaries also facilitated free transfers of foreign currencies, as well as complete anonymity.

By these means the profit figures reported by the company could continuously be massaged upwards to bring about a sharp rise in the share price. If any unit incurred losses, this information was not shown publicly, but camouflaged in different ways.

During Lay's time Enron was made to look substantially more profitable than it actually was, but it started a vicious circle. In the heated economic environment of the 1990s, the eagerly expected quarterly corporate results had to be manipulated all the time through ever more imaginative financial tricks.

The Enron management created an illusion of billion-dollar profits, although the company in reality lost money all the time.

Enron's rise to stardom started in the first half of the 1990s. It was propelled by the US Congress' decision to liberate the electricity markets. In this freewheeling market environment, Enron exploited the violent fluctuations in electricity price.

The company had close ties with the political decision-makers, including two presidents, father and son Bush. It contributed actively to campaign financing. The efficient lobbying served the company's strategy beautifully. Enron's comet-like expansion went on and on, and in 2000 it had already become the seventh largest company in the US.

Enron's Glossy Picture – and the Truth

Enron's top management was of course well aware of the decisive role played by the offshore firms in hiding any losses. But investors, banks, media and stock analysts did not yet suspect anything. When *Fortune* magazine published its Fortune 500 list of the largest companies in the US, Enron was flatteringly rated among the ten best.

The dishonest accounting practices were of course particularly focused on jacking up the share price to ever higher levels. Lay and the company's other directors had no qualms about using inside information in their profitable personal trades in Enron stocks.

Lay had seen to it that he was one of the highest paid chief executives in the US. In 1999 he received a royal compensation package of $42.4 million (about $55 million today).

At his peak, Lay was held in high esteem in wide circles, to the point that in December 2000 he was even mentioned as a possible candidate for the secretary of the treasury job in President George W. Bush's cabinet. The rumour attested to Lay's excellent political contacts and his generous grants to the Republican Party.

Kenneth Lay's Smart Accomplices

One of Lay's closest collaborators was Andrew Fastow, who acted as Enron's chief financial officer. He was in charge of the intricate off-balance-sheet company network, and manipulated deals from which he himself, his family and friends pocketed hundreds of millions of dollars in safe profits, at the expense of the company he worked for and its stockholders.

Fastow was definitely not as pure as the driven snow. Before moving to Enron he had innovated a new capital acquisition scheme in the Continental Illinois National Bank and Trust Company, located in Chicago.

The bank started to raise additional capital by selling securities, backed by risky loans, to investors – in a similar manner as before the recent US banking crisis. The new idea also caught on elsewhere within the banking sector. It moved assets off the bank's balance sheet while creating revenue. At the same time as it reduced the balance sheet, it could secure capital on favourable terms.

The Continental Bank ran into problems precisely because of this dubious practice, partly because some of the risky loans backfired. It was the largest financial institution to disappear from the US banking map during the previous American banking crisis at the turn of the 1980s and 1990s.

Another of Lay's dubious subordinates was Jeffrey Skilling, chief executive of EnronOnline, which was established in 1999. It was an Internet-based trading company used by almost every American energy company.

As the chief architect of the company's aggressive action plan, Skilling made Enron the largest wholesale seller of gas and electricity in the United States. During the best quarter in 2000, its sales rose to an impressive $27 billion.

Skilling introduced a completely new way of thinking within Enron: on its balance sheet there was no need for that large assets. Under this new, debatable accounting practice, the estimated future sales profits were booked in advance, as if they had already been paid. On this basis Enron also registered profits emanating from uncertain claims, although eventually they might turn out to be loss-making or not even materialise at all.

The restoration of Enron's financial health was resolutely put in the background, and the main focus continued to be to inflate the share price further during Wall Street's IT boom in the late 1990s. Thanks to the incessant surge of its shares, fresh money flowed into Enron in a steady stream from both investors and banks.

The debt-laden Enron rode forward on the crest of this money wave. The company's management knew, however, that if the share price were to turn southward, their house of cards would collapse.

Share Price Collapses and Investors Flee

At the end of the 1990s Enron's share had climbed to new phenomenal peaks of between $80 and $90. Until then only a few observers worried about the peculiar lack of transparency in the accounts, but little by little financial analysts started to wake up.

Still, in July 2001, the high-flying Enron reported $50.1 billion in revenue for the previous 12-month period. This represented a huge improvement compared with the previous year. Despite this, the company's profit margin turned out to be a disappointing 2.1 per cent, and the share had dropped by 30 per cent from the summer of 2000.

Enron's setbacks continued to accumulate. It ran into tremendous operational problems, among other things, with the trading unit's logistics which were broadband operated, and with the huge Dabhol Power station in India. The management was also busy trying to calm public outrage against the company in California during the energy crisis in 2000–2001.

The first one to jump ship in August 2001 was Enron's chief executive, Jeffrey Skilling. He had served Enron for only six months. Market rumours had it that Skilling sold at least 450,000 shares in the months preceding his departure. Their sale price was about $33 million. He was still left with over one million shares.

Chairman Kenneth Lay tried to calm the stock analysts by assuring, with a straight face, that "there would be no changes in the performance or outlook of the company going forward". He also affirmed that there was "absolutely no accounting issue, no trading issue, no reserve issue, no previously unknown problem issues" prompting Skilling's departure. Simultaneously, Lay announced that he would again take charge as CEO.

Despite these comforting words investors continued to dump Enron's shares, causing a new sharp slide in the share. In this situation, analysts became increasingly alarmed because neither the company's business nor its accounts were opened up to outside observers. It was impossible to decipher whether Enron ran a profit or lost money. The stock was trading under a cloud.

The confident Lay admitted that the mighty Enron's operations were quite complicated. But that was mainly due to its sophisticated tax strategy as well as to its hedging of interest rate and other positions against risks.

In October 2001 Enron's management was finally forced to announce some shattering news: the company had incurred staggering losses of over $1 billion in the third quarter, due to investment losses, along with various charges. Lay also reported that some new investment losses were on the horizon.

After these bad tidings stock analysts climbed the walls. On top of everything, the SEC announced that it would start investigating some suspicious deals struck by Enron. The share collapsed to a low of $20.

Lay quickly called a press conference where he announced that Chief Financial Officer Andrew Fastow had been sent packing "in order to restore investor confidence". The same Fastow who had been one of Lay's closest confidants.

Lay underlined that for many years one of the world's best accounting firms, Arthur Andersen, had scrutinised Enron's financial and accounting practices, and had found no cause for serious concerns.

Delaying Tactics and Bankruptcy

In an effort to remove any doubts about Enron's cash position, the company began buying back all its short-term commercial papers, valued at around $3.3 billion. It financed the repurchases by using up its lines of credit at several banks.

The vicious circle spun rapidly towards a catastrophe. The witch-hunt was on. Numerous companies that had agreements with Enron started to fear serious trouble if Enron's credit rating were downgraded. When

the two leading rating agencies in the world, Moody's and Standard &
Poor's, indeed lowered Enron's rating, it was almost a deadly blow as clients,
investors and banks started to evade Enron. The collapse of the share just
accelerated, and in November 2001, it dropped to barely $7.

The desperate Lay and his underlings tried to find a buyer for the
company. The preliminary talks with a smaller energy trading company,
Dynegy, had been promising, but no final agreement was reached. Enron's
credit rating fell to junk level or even lower. Fewer and fewer companies
were willing to risk trading with Enron.

The credibility and reputation of the company's management were
further blackened by additional revelations: before the crisis Lay himself
and several directors had sold shares for several hundred million dollars
– although Lay had warmly recommended the shares to his staff for some
time after that.

Thousands of Enron's employees were devastated to see their
retirement savings, which primarily comprised Enron shares, devalued by
90 per cent in one year alone. The most shattering loss by a single employee
rose to over $800,000.

Finally, in November 2001, Enron's top management was forced to
admit that the situation was desperate because it would have to amortise
an astonishing $9 billion of its gigantic debts before the end of 2002. Such
an almost unimaginable debt service burden "was vastly in excess" of its
available cash.

The flames were further fanned as the deal with Dynegy failed, and
Lay had to admit that all the money borrowed recently (including the sums
allocated for the repurchase of commercial paper) had been used up within
a mere 50 days.

The SEC announced that it had filed a civil fraud complaint against
Enron's auditor, Arthur Andersen. As if this was not enough: fearing the
risks connected with Enron, most of the remaining clients started to leave
for competing firms.

The share crashed to an all-time low of 61 cents, compared with a peak of $90. Enron's debts were a hair-raising $23 billion (about $28 billion today). Two large banks in particular, Citigroup and J. P. Morgan, ran serious default risks as most of Enron's assets were tied up as security to other creditors.

The end result was the most expensive bankruptcy in the history of the United States. In addition, 4,000 people lost their jobs.

To add insult to injury, the grief-stricken employees were given merely 30 minutes to pack their belongings and leave the Houston head office after this sad news was announced.

Heavy Charges

The estate inventory by the bankruptcy trustees and the consideration of charges took several years. The trial started only in January 2006. Those principally accused were board chairman Kenneth Lay, the short-term chief executive, Jeffrey Skilling, and the chief financial officer, Andrew Fastow.

A long list of charges was read to Kenneth Lay. The impressive 65-page indictment included 11 counts of securities fraud, wire fraud, making false and misleading statements, money laundering, conspiracy and insider trading. It was generally surmised that he would receive a jail sentence of at least 25 to 30 years. The SEC demanded over $90 million in damages from him, in addition to the fines.

Lay refuted all the charges. He insisted that he had been misled by his colleagues, and that there was "a conspiracy" waged by short-sellers, rogue executives and the media.

In May 2006 he was found guilty on six counts of conspiracy and fraud by a jury of eight women and four men. Sentencing was scheduled to take place in September 2006. However, Lay died at age 64 of a heart attack during a vacation in Colorado in July 2006.

Despite his short time at Enron, chief executive Skilling was severely punished with 24 years and four months of jail. Moreover, he was sentenced to pay $26 million in damages to the Enron pension fund.

The slippery Andrew Fastow, who had been the mastermind behind the offshore deception companies and questionable accounting practices, volunteered to assist the prosecutor and the deferral authorities. As the star witness against his former boss and colleagues, he got away with only six years of jail, and will be released in 2011.

Kenneth Lay had been married for 22 years to his second wife, his former secretary Linda Lay. They had two children, three adopted children and 12 grandchildren. During the trial it emerged that wife Linda had sold about 500,000 Enron shares only a few minutes before the news concerning the collapse of the firm was published. No charges were brought against her.

Political Connections and Demise of Arthur Andersen

Later revelations confirmed that Enron had been enormously active in political lobbying, with a view to steering energy legislation and supervision by the authorities in the "right direction" from Enron's point of view. After 1990, it was estimated that the company had invested some $7 million into politics.

The Republican Party received the main part of Lay's and Enron's substantial donations. Nobody was surprised to learn that an impressive crowd of 1,200 people, including former President George H. W. Bush, attended Lay's memorial service in 2006 in Houston.

During Bill Clinton's presidencies, Enron and Kenneth Lay donated a total of $900,000 to the Democratic Party. Besides this friendly aid, the company donated in 1999 and 2000 the sum of $362,000 in so-called soft money to the Democratic Party. This money could not be used for supporting political candidates.

Another big corpse in the Enron scandal was Arthur Andersen. In 2002 it was found guilty of obstruction of justice as it had destroyed a great deal of documents related to its audit work on Enron.

The global success story of the great Arthur Andersen company ended. Its network had 28,000 employees in the US alone, and 85,000 elsewhere in the world. Following the scandal, the accounting and audit legislation in many countries was further tightened.

At its peak, well before the bankruptcy, the market value (market cap) of Enron, one of the world's largest energy companies, had been a staggering $68 billion. Many Enron shareholders lost almost everything, and thousands of employees at least $1 billion of their pension savings.

The investors who brought lawsuits against Enron estimated that the accounting crimes cost at least $25 billion in losses.

WINCAPITA'S
MULTIMILLION DOLLAR
PYRAMID

Investment club WinCapita has been investigated by the National Bureau of Investigation ("Finland's FBI") since March 2008. It is suspected of having run an extensive fraud scheme involving about 10,000 persons who in total invested over €100 million (about $130 million). The estimated damages are over €41 million.

The WinCapita case has excited wide public interest because it seems to represent a classic and ingenious pyramid, the largest Ponzi-style pyramid swindle ever in the Nordic countries.

The principal suspect, Hannu Kailajärvi, was born in Finland in 1962. He graduated from a technical institute with a degree in computer science. In 1989 he opened a restaurant with his wife, but it went bankrupt four years later. Their next venture was a music bar, which was later transformed into an erotic restaurant.

This tireless entrepreneur moved to a new field in 1997, starting the Nefernet web-marketing firm, which also sold telephone cards. It advertised selling phone calls at half the price of that in the large phone companies. The restaurant was declared insolvent in 2000 and failed in 2002.

Kailajärvi and some of his collaborators started their first investment club, WinClub, in 2005. Its activities may have been negatively affected by founder Kailajärvi's six-month suspended jail sentence in 2006 for breach of trust and accounting crimes. As there were also some critical TV stories about WinClub, the name was changed in 2007 to WinCapita, probably in order to continue on a clean slate.

Gradual Build-Up of the Pyramid

The suspected WinCapita fraud became public in March 2008. The National Bureau of Investigation had monitored WinCapita's web marketing and investment activities for some time, but only at that point did the police feel it had sufficient proof that WinCapita had not engaged in any of its advertised super-profitable foreign exchange trading, through which the investors would receive their rich returns. The police concluded that the WinCapita investment club probably represented criminal activities.

Its predecessor, WinClub, had around 2005 already established a foreign fronting firm, Worldwide Investment Company, first in Florida, but later as a registered offshore paper company in Panama. It was supposed to develop WinClub products and services.

It must be stressed that in pyramid cases the suspects, the complainants and the witnesses frequently tell quite different "truths" in police interrogations because these cases involve large sums of money and accusations of major crime.

Pyramids are complicated to investigate since thousands of people have to be questioned and the fraud techniques are elaborate. Usually they involve both domestic and international firms and money transfers to tax havens. The testimonies presented in courts are often equally contradictory. Besides outright securities fraud, tax, accounting and foreign exchange crimes have often also been committed.

To reinforce the club's credibility, WinClub allegedly opened a bank account in the large Crédit Suisse bank. Its web page was soon moved to the hard-to-track Root eSolutions, a provider of Internet services located in

Luxembourg. The club's money transfers were handled by Moneybookers, a British e-commerce firm.

The WinCapita case can, in several regards, be compared to Ponzi's pyramid structure. Ponzi promised immense profits to his investors, he did not do any of the alleged businesses, and the investments were marketed by an energetic army of bonus-driven sales agents.

Ponzi argued that he could generate his huge returns by buying and selling international postal reply coupons, while WinClub and WinCapita said the great profits came from speculative trade in foreign exchange. In reality, neither of them (nor Ponzi) did any genuine background business except collecting money from investors under false pretences.

Bonus-Driven Agents to Work at Full Speed

Both WinCapita and its predecessor WinClub were skilfully designed to look as tempting as possible. With the help of the "brilliant" foreign exchange speculation model that they claimed to have invented, they allegedly held out hopes of up to 260 to 400 per cent profits per annum to investors.

In an effort to keep unwanted people (perhaps the likes of journalists, securities analysts or bank professionals) outside, membership in the club could be gained only on the recommendation of the numerous sales agents known as sponsors or other members. The agents played a crucial role in building up the scheme and were spurred on by generous introduction fees or by sharing members' profits.

The first-comers were paid rich "investment profits" directly into their bank accounts. By bragging about these high returns and even flashing bank statements confirming them, they created a convincing picture of the club. Even the most sceptical could see in black and white that the system worked beautifully, that it was a "piece of cake".

The introduction fees paid to the sponsors were probably fairly easy money, as long as they attracted many new members. A marketing paper attributed to WinClub stated that if a sponsoring club member enrolled five new members, he would receive 20 per cent of their profits. If he then convinced these five individuals to invest €10,000 each, and if each of them really received the envisaged return of €13,000 in six months (at the rate of 260 per cent per annum proposed in the paper), the sponsor's share was 20 per cent of a total of €65,000, meaning €13,000.

In all likelihood many sponsors and members did not leave the profits on their personal bank accounts because they were so convinced of the superiority of WinClub's/WinCapita's investment scheme, having witnessed the constant inflow of "profits". As their greediness grew, they typically reinvested their profits and fees into the club to reap even more fancy returns. For this reason the profits and fees paid to them did not strain the club's liquidity.

Although the more than €100-million investments in WinClub, and later WinCapita, were mostly paid directly into these companies' bank accounts, some investors evidently paid their stakes in cash to the sales agents, perhaps partly to conceal the true origin of the money. It may have represented "grey" money left unreported in income tax returns, drug money or money laundering. Some sales agents may even have refrained from passing on the money to the clubs and instead put it in their own pockets.

As always in pyramids, the major part of the "profits" went to fairly few persons. Of the 10,000 members, only about 350 accounts received money transfers exceeding €50,000. Of those same 350 investors, one half (175 in all) were lucky to get over €100,000 and six over €1 million.

The 500 investors who registered the largest gains got altogether €68 million of the total €94 million paid out to all members during 2005–2008. Consequently, a mere five per cent of all the members was credited with over 70 per cent of the money paid out by the clubs to members' accounts.

The Psychology of Swindling People

In our funny world, numerous people feel that they are unique, more capable, smarter than the average. They sincerely think they deserve something better in life, better than others.

WinCapita's message surely appealed to man's inherent egoism: they thought it was fantastic that somebody expressly contacted *you,* offering *you* rich profits, a personalised promise about well-deserved quick enrichment.

According to Hannu Lauerma, head physician of the Prison Mental Hospital in Helsinki, people are flattered by being invited to an inner circle, a closed private society. Being an insider boosts peoples' appreciation of their own importance. Besides, a member of a private society is somebody who knows more.

The success of pyramid swindlers is also due to the fact that they do *not* have to convince large masses of people who may take a critical attitude. Even if only one per cent, or even one in a thousand people, swallows the bait, they can collect millions.

WinCapita's credibility was bolstered because the sponsors soliciting investments were often locally respected people or even family members, friends, fellow believers, business associates or others sharing the same hobbies. Or the sponsors referred to well-known persons who had already put money into the scheme, perhaps even pocketed nice profits.

Fathers recommended investments to their sons, or sons to fathers, workmates to workmates, the faithful to fellow believers, neighbour to neighbour, or a jogger to his sporting companion. Many went along also because of neighbourly envy, having learnt that the guy next door had earned great profits and gone on a binge on foreign sun-drenched beaches.

Background of WinCapita's Victims

WinCapita collected money from people with basic greed, who dreamt about a better life. Some of them were also addicted to money games and betting.

WinCapita's members came from all walks of life. They included insurance agents, carpenters, electricians, gas station owners, farmers, entrepreneurs who had sold their businesses and a number of Pentecostalists and other believers.

According to financial journalist Antti Mikkonen, WinCapita's marketing agents slandered the banks, arguing that "the banks are bullshitting their clients". This picture was psychologically infectious. The mumbo jumbo of banks' investment managers, with their offers of a measly one or two per cent deposit interest, did not catch on when a brother, friend, cousin or colleague had boasted about his 100 per cent profits.

Thousands of investors flocked to WinCapita from all over the country. Most had received information about WinCapita through word of mouth since the club rules stipulated that members were prohibited from giving information to the media without its written permission. Even web pages and web discussion forums were covered by this ban.

Members' Fees and Currency Signal System

WinClub's alleged information material to members and investors seems incoherent. The large daily newspaper, *Aamulehti*, came across a presentation which seems to have only one objective: to attract a maximum of new investments into the pyramid, with no questions asked.

According to the Club's rules, the entry fee for members was €3,000. That was the minimum investment. However, the recommended "sensible minimum", was €5,000 (about $6,500 today). For most small investors these sums represented fairly substantial stakes but, on the other hand, the appreciable entry fee gave it a professional image.

The minimum stake entitled the member to a basic licence and the right to make foreign exchange investments and to recommend new members (which produced substantial rewards). Many members invested much more than the minimum.

The text even claimed: "There are also bigger investors (over €100,000). The participation of major investors brings reliability into the activities; a professional investor does not put up any money unless he is sure that the scheme will fly."

The marketing of pyramid investments is always based on something particularly eye-catching, but at the same time, difficult to understand. In Ponzi's case it was the international arbitrage in postal reply coupons, and in WinCapita, it was the FxTrader Signals system.

The system supposedly showed buying and selling signals for the dollar and the euro in real time. The club and its members, it was suggested, could exploit these signals in their own forex speculation.

Some members were under the impression that the club's FxTrader Signals system showed foreign exchange trades actually made by the club. However, Kailajärvi's confession to the police corrected this misunderstanding. He said that the programme only copied the foreign exchange curves for the euro and the dollar, and just added various buying and selling signals.

Evidently very few of the members took the time, or had the background needed, to familiarise themselves with the scheme from a critical viewpoint. A natural question would have been: if the currency signals system was so ingenious and hyper-profitable, why was it not used elsewhere by the big banks and corporations?

Other questions: how was it possible that WinCapita's management, which evidently had little or no experience in foreign exchange trading, had succeeded in developing such a perpetual motion earnings machine, when global foreign exchange experts had not been able to do the same? Why did the club not sell such a possibly even Nobel Prize-winning invention for top dollars to the world?

One final question: if WinCapita really possessed such a revolutionary financial invention, why did its sales agents bother to roam the countryside from house to house to collect money from grandpas and grandmas?

In the initial police interrogations, the principal accused, Kailajärvi, already confessed that the company itself had not traded at all in foreign exchange, although that was supposed to provide such attractive business income. It was all a fake. The talk about such profitable forex speculation was only an enticing lure to attract money from members.

Basically the same method used by billion-dollar swindler Bernard Madoff in the US.

Messy Marketing Information

Other marketing information on the Internet proclaimed that a VIP member could trade in four different categories through the FxTrader Signals system: A, B, C and X. Of the VIP member's €3,000 membership fee, €1,000 was the basic stake, the minimum investment in forex trading was €1,000, and the third €1,000 gave the member the right to recommend new members.

The reader was informed that during the last two years, WinClub had managed to achieve about 5 per cent in weekly profits in its forex trading – which on a straight line basis (without reinvestments) would equal 260 per cent per year.

Anybody with a foreign exchange background surely knows that it is practically impossible to achieve such profits continuously week to week in real risk inherent forex trading, anywhere other than in WinClub's marketing material. WinClub itself did not even have its own foreign exchange trading room, so let alone many members.

More strange information to investors:

"The value of the VIP members' joint X-return account determines the maximum investment per cent for the X-series' licensed share purchases. The figure is calculated every 13 weeks (sic). There's also a formula for calculating the investment per cent: $P = Z + (C/20,000)$, where P is the new investment per cent, Z the previous investment per cent, and C is the value of the profit account."

The formula looks completely nonsensical, a pure bluff, and it is hard to see that anything sensible could be calculated on that basis.

Even if the unintelligible formula lulled some investors into believing that it represented a brilliant new invention, others may have suspected that WinClub's and WinCapita's managers had enjoyed themselves thoroughly when they created such a hilarious "formula".

According to the text, the profit forecast for 12 months from an initial €10,000 investment capital, assuming regular reinvestments, would be the princely sum of €53,257. Consequently, the one-year profit would amount to 433 per cent.

The text writers even dared to state that "foreign exchange trading is quite sustainable in relation to global economic disturbances". Again, anybody with an interest in foreign exchange knows that market volatility is exceptionally high and may result in enormous losses, as witnessed by the billion-dollar forex and derivative scandals within Baring Brothers, Société Générale and many other financial institutions.

And more bizarre rules:

"The VIP-members will be granted member recommendation fees as follows: 20 per cent of the basic license sales price for the signal system, 10 per cent of the sales price for the license shares sold to clients, 5 per cent of the sales price for the FxTrader Autopilot systems sold to clients, 2.5 per cent of the profits on the client's or member's foreign exchange trading and 20 per cent of the Forex Pool profits earned by the members they have sponsored."

All this may look serious on the surface. But the concept is strange since it seems unlikely that more than a handful of the members did any forex trading at all on the basis of the FxTrader Autopilot. And if so, they would hardly have reported their profits to the clubs. Again it seems that the rule was not meant to be comprehensible.

Despite its incoherence, thousands of investors trusted that the system was ingenious as they were promised such rich returns. They were more than happy to recommend the scheme and enrol additional investors.

Nothing new under the sun: the earlier-mentioned great swindler, Sir John Blunt, already had as his maxim in the 1700s' South Sea scheme – "The more confusion the better."

Gains and Suicides

A group of people who had been involved in WinCapita met in February 2009. The media reported that these former members sincerely hoped that the club's operations would be restarted soonest, and most of them certainly did not feel that they had been swindled.

In a TV 4 newscast the spokesman for the group lamented that the police investigation was "a conspiracy within the Ministry of the Interior, which directed the police investigations". Furthermore he regretted that the publicity about WinCapita "had already led to eight suicides".

To judge from the heart-warming comments from the meeting, the participants had good memories of WinCapita, for instance, because they had had the sense to cash in their profits early, or had made a bundle through their sales agent fees and commissions. Some of them may genuinely have considered WinCapita a sound idea, ruined by the police through their abrupt intervention.

Nothing in the life of man changes rapidly. In the same way as in the Poyais phantom state swindle in the early 1800s, where part of the fooled emigrants accused the newspapers of libel and false reporting, the

WinCapita meeting 200 years later criticised the police for "confusing and biased information".

The truth of the matter is of course that the police intervention saved a lot of old and new victims from smarting losses.

However, in the spring of 2010, a number of WinCapita's former members held a new meeting and expressed their hope that the scheme would be restarted. Evidently this meeting was also mainly attended by earlier net winners.

WinCapita's Massive Police Investigation

WinClub's and later WinCapita's web pages ran for about three years altogether. But without any advance warning, WinCapita's web page was closed in March 2008, and the truth started to dawn.

Those who considered that they had been swindled by the WinCapita scheme could sign up with the authorities as injured parties in a class-action lawsuit, and demand compensation from the perpetrators for their damages. There were about ten main suspects, but legal experts believe that some sponsors may also be sued for aiding and abetting. The police arrested the main suspect in December 2008 and some other suspects in March 2009.

The police estimated that the total investments made into the club since 2005 was about €100 million. WinCapita paid back €32.6 million in January–March 2008. These sums went mainly to the club's early members, who cashed in their stakes.

But thousands of Finns were left with heavy losses. By the stipulated deadline in mid-2009, about 2,600 complainants had signed up with the police. Their reported damage claims were about €32 million. The assets sequestrated by the police came up to about €17 million.

The Finnish tax authorities have tentatively concluded that members' "investments" in WinCapita did not represent any genuine capital investments, rather only account transfers. Therefore, the painful losses incurred by thousands of members will probably not be deductible in their capital gains taxation, unlike capital losses from equity investments, for instance. This is further bad news for many WinCapita victims.

Interestingly enough only about one quarter of all the 10,000 investors filed a complaint, even if it is highly unlikely that the others did not incur any losses at all.

There are probably other reasons. Many investors may not have wanted to contact the police because their losses were minor or because they feared the publicity at the trial – that it would be widely known that they had allowed themselves to be cheated. Others may not have wanted to disclose the origins of their invested funds.

The investigation by the National Bureau of Investigation, as well as the interrogations of the suspects and thousands of investors, has been very time-consuming. Compared with other crimes, where there is usually only one or, at most, a few suspects, this legal case is completely different as there are huge numbers of victims. The police interrogated 3,200 people, and the pre-trial material adds up to 5,200 pages, plus numerous videotapes.

The police also pointed out that a lot of money circulated in both directions, to the point that WinCapita's bank statements alone did not even fit into one single van. There were also international connections.

The highly publicised trial started only in late 2010 and will continue into 2011. It is the largest in Finland's history. The public prosecutor has requested a jail sentence of at least five years for main suspect Kailajärvi, who, according to the prosecution, gained over €6 million.

In addition, besides interrogating the original suspects and hearing a large number of complainants, the police have started to interrogate several hundred of the investors who received substantial profits from WinCapita, or did not claim compensation for their losses.

Besides the thousands of complainants and other members of

Wincapita, the process is closely followed by tens of thousands of family members and friends and, of course, by the general public in Finland and in the other Nordic countries. The main trial commenced in early 2011.

16

THE CRIMINAL OF
THE CENTURY

Today's world is a strange mixed-up place. Not even in their wildest dreams could anybody imagine that the great American investment guru, Bernard Madoff, would get 150 years in jail and the dubious title of "Criminal of the Century".

As Madoff confessed his world-record Ponzi pyramid swindle in late 2008, the whole investment world was flabbergasted. It shattered the traditional rules of trust in serious portfolio investing, which had become so immensely popular during the stock market booms of the 1990s and early 2000s.

Nothing will be the same after America's largest financial fraud ever, committed by a superstar of the investment fund sector. Rich portfolio investors will not easily forget Madoff, as it is said that money has the memory of an elephant – besides the courage of a hare and the speed of a gazelle.

Thousands of the unsuspecting rich and super-rich gladly steered billions of dollars into Madoff's house of cards, without doing the normal prudent due diligence. On their part, the investment fund managers who fed Madoff's treacherous fund with billions were blinded by their exorbitant commissions.

Madoff's Early Life

Bernard Lawrence "Bernie" Madoff became filthy rich, but he came from a fairly humble background. He was born in New York's Queens to a Jewish family in 1938. His father, Ralph Z., first worked as a plumber before becoming a stockbroker, and his mother, Sylvia Madoff, also worked in their small brokerage firm. The SEC investigated the company in the 1960s for failing to fulfil its financial reporting.

Madoff graduated from Hofstra University in October 1960 with a degree in political science. He also passed a licensing test allowing him to deal in securities. Madoff liked to promote the myth that he had a law degree, but he never graduated from any law school although he took some law classes.

As a beach lifeguard and sprinkler-fitter, the young Madoff saved about $5,000. With this money and $50,000 (over $350,000 in today's money) borrowed from his in-laws, he founded a small Wall Street broker-dealer firm in 1960. He traded in cheap, small company shares as a penny stock trader.

Bernie married Ruth Madoff (née Alpern) in 1959. She had graduated with a degree in psychology from Queen's College and started to work next to him in their own firm. At first they did not do very well, but it all took off with the help of his father-in-law, Saul (Sol) Alpern. The well-connected accountant recommended Madoff to his rich friends, who spent the winter in Florida and the summer in the Catskill Mountains.

From then on, Madoff's career advanced under a lucky star.

The wealthy Madoff's posh apartment on Manhattan's East Side was valued at $7 million in 2009. His summer retreat was in Montauk on the east point of Long Island's Atlantic coast.

Madoff also had a luxurious apartment home in Cap d'Antibes on the French Riviera, and a 27-metre (89 foot) long Leopard yacht named *The Bull*. It was moored in the nearby harbour of Port Gallice and was valued at $7 million.

On top of all this the Madoffs owned an $11 million, almost 900 square metre imposing mansion in Florida's Palm Beach. It had earlier housed the famous Pulitzer family.

Madoff and his wife were members of the exclusive Palm Beach Country Club, home of millionaires and other celebrities. There they played golf and socialised.

In his profession Madoff always appeared stylishly dressed in expensive, tailor-made grey suits and silk ties.

The enterprising and bright Bernard Madoff saw the opportunities opened up in the investment field by the new information technology quite early. He started to use rapid data technology in his brokerage business, and his clients liked the fast information and the quick and punctual deals.

In this way, Madoff was able to bypass the established Wall Street houses and their antiquated auction system. He revolutionised equity trading and made it more democratic. At the same time he also made a lot of enemies among the big broker-dealers who jealously guarded their territory.

After a few years and some initial technical hiccups, a few broker-dealers, including Madoff, started up the NASDAQ, the stock exchange for new technology, in 1971. Nasdaq stands for National Association for Securities Dealers Automated Quotations. It is now one of the largest trading venues in the world. The Nasdaq exchange operates in New York and deals in 3,300 firms. Many of them are new and rapidly growing.

At one stage, Madoff's firm was the largest market participant in Nasdaq's equity trading. On these merits he was elected board chairman of Nasdaq which, of course, cemented his reputation among important investors.

Already in the 1970s, Madoff came up with the idea to pay commissions to outside fund managers who directed equity deals to his firm. It was tantamount to a legal kickback, a generous one per cent, and later, up to four per cent to some feeder funds. These commissions made many broker-dealers and fund managers rich and happy to work with Madoff.

Using this questionable practice, Madoff achieved a 5 to 15 per cent share of the total equity trading volume on the New York Stock Exchange. In 2008 he was the sixth largest market maker on Wall Street.

Most observers believe that Madoff's monumental scam started only in the mid-1990s – as he himself claimed. However, some US government investigators maintain that he had already started swindling in the 1980s.

Behind the Facade of the Head Office

Bernard L. Madoff Investment Securities' corporate headquarters was located in the 34-floor Lipstick Building right in the centre of Manhattan, at 885 Third Avenue. His company occupied three floors.

The Lipstick Building was partly owned by Madoff's long-time friend, Fred Wilpon. He is known as part-owner of the famous New York Mets baseball club. Swindled by his close friend, Wilpon also suffered heavy losses.

Madoff himself worked on the top 19th floor, together with his brother Peter, and Madoff's two sons, Mark and Andrew, as well as a secretary. This floor was mainly occupied by about 40 to 50 traders, who were not involved in Madoff's treacherous activities. They traded with institutions, while the investment advisory unit (better known as the Ponzi) dealt only with private persons, according to financial journalist Mark Seal of *Vanity Fair* magazine.

The legal securities dealing acted as a "Potemkin village", fooling the authorities and investors into believing that everything was normal. The huge pyramid swindle was perpetrated behind this facade. Many meetings with large investors were held with the market-making trading room as a backdrop. They saw the busy trading floor with their own eyes and thought that everything was normal.

Ruth Madoff occupied a large office on the 18th floor, which she visited a few times a week. The same floor also housed some lawyers, the internal audit, the IT outfit and the small investment firm, Cohmad Securities, mainly owned by Maurice Cohn. The name Cohmad was taken from the names Cohn and Madoff. It lured a lot of rich investors into Madoff's trap. It also acted as the Madoff family's personal bank.

Below that, on the 17th floor, was the investment advisory outfit. At the same time as Madoff made himself a name for revolutionising the stock trading on Wall Street, he gradually built up his secret advisory business. It was supposedly handling Madoff's major private clients' investments, and registered the fabricated profits on the accounts of his hedge fund.

The whole advisory unit employed 17 fairly inexperienced, lowly-paid young women, who were not very educated and without any broad experience in the financial sector. They were instructed to write confirmations (tickets) for share purchases, which in reality had not been made, and they did what they were told to do. The young ladies delivered summaries of these fictitious "investments" made in the name of the clients to Madoff. The unit was headed by Annette Bongiorno.

Madoff took a nonchalant attitude towards the authorities. He did not even bother to submit his registration as an investment adviser with the SEC before it became mandatory in 2006, despite the fact that he had been active in the field for many years and on a large scale. However, nobody questioned this omission.

Perhaps one explanation for this deliberate negligence was that the SEC owed him a lot. Madoff's vast expertise in the markets was much admired and respected among SEC staff. Already in the 1970s and 1980s, Madoff had helped the SEC in their quest to implement more competition in the markets. Madoff's name was so well known in the SEC that in some matters he probably had been able to influence its policies.

Madoff probably felt that he could get away with the phoney advisory business cum hedge fund as long as it stayed out of sight. Hardly anybody saw it in actual practice. The acclaimed investigative reporter Erin Arvedlund, in her well-researched book on Madoff, which is referred to in this chapter, states that "he literally operated right under the noses of the SEC market regulators".

What's A Hedge Fund?

The original American "Hedged Fund" was invented by the sociologist, Alfred Winslow Jones, in 1949. He made bets on stocks and other securities which he believed were going up in price ("long positions") and at the same time wagered on stocks going down in price ("short positions"). The general idea was that if the overall markets rose, the loss on shorted assets would be more than cancelled by the additional gain on assets bought, and vice versa.

In this way the portfolio would be a profitable "hedged fund".

The explosive increase of the hedge fund industry is illustrated by the fact that there are now some 8,500 hedge fund firms in operation, more than all the public companies trading on the New York Stock Exchange. In comparison, in 1985 only 68 hedge fund firms were in existence.

A hedge fund manager will typically charge fees of "2 and 20". That refers to the standard management fee of 2 per cent of the fund's net asset value each year, and the standard performance fee of 20 per cent of the fund's profit, normally counting both realised and unrealised profits. But within the whole hedge fund sector the management fee ranges between 1 and 4 per cent per annum, while the performance fee range is from 10 up to an astounding 40 to 50 per cent.

As hedge funds were not required to register with the SEC until 2006, Madoff could, for a long time, operate freely without the supervising authorities questioning what he was doing. It gave him the cover of exclusivity and secrecy that he needed.

The Keys to Madoff's Appeal

My personal summary of how Madoff's skilfully executed approach differed from rudimentary Ponzis (for instance, Charles Ponzi's own or WinCapita's) is as follows:

1. Madoff's operations succeeded for such a long time because he had an excellent reputation on Wall Street as an astute broker-dealer and former board chairman of Nasdaq. He was admired by millionaires and investors alike as an innovative investment guru.

2. Madoff did not boast about ultra-high 100 to 400 per cent profits a year. He typically promised some 10 to 15 per cent returns from year to year, like clockwork, come rain or shine. Such moderation, combined with stable profits, appealed to the experienced rich investors and reinforced their confidence.

3. Madoff wooed wealthy individuals or charities in a discreet way. He never overplayed his hand, and did not openly fish for investments, in contrast to many hard-sell firms. He chose his investors carefully; often they were large feeder funds which supplemented his own natural investor base.

4. His fund was not open to the masses. This selective strategy just reinforced Madoff's appeal. His trick of rejecting certain investors, giving the impression of not needing their money, worked marvellously. Many rich investors openly begged to become a client in this exclusive and desirable fund.

5. The fund's investment strategy was protected as a proprietary secret. It was allegedly sophisticated, consistent and safe, but "too complicated for outsiders to understand".

6. Well aware of the stinginess of many rich people, Madoff did not charge the usual expensive investment fund fees and commissions. He said that "Jews like a discount." The millionaires were enamoured by Madoff's no-charge policy. He only charged small trading commissions. The clients believed that he earned his business income from securities trading.

7. Madoff was a master illusionist. He was able to hide his Ponzi for at least 15 to 20 years, contrary to most other swindlers who make big mistakes or follow the "hit and run strategy".

8. Madoff portrayed himself as cautious and discreet, which appealed to rich investors. In contrast to other hedge funds, his clients had to sign confidentiality agreements, committing themselves not to talk about the firm or reveal that they were invested with him.

One Madoff investor underlined to Arvedlund that:

> "Part of the Jewish mentality is prudence, especially financial prudence, conservatism, not taking risks. Madoff was the opposite of risk – he was anti-risk... He played to that sense of conservatism, that he was not a get-rich-quick scam."

Madoff also made a name for himself on Capitol Hill as a generous political donor to both the Democratic and Republican Parties' election campaigns, and as an aggressive lobbyist for stock market restructuring. He sat on a number of committees in his field.

Secret Investment Strategy

How was this world-record fraud executed in actual practice? How is it possible that thousands of experienced and wealthy businessmen and other millionaires, many renowned investment funds in the US, Europe, South America and Asia, and large charities handling billions of dollars, fell for it?

Madoff's long and successful swindling story is almost incredible – but unfortunately true.

In the Bernard L. Madoff Investment Securities sales pitches to investors, Madoff outlined his "split-strike conversion strategy" as such: that he took positions in 30 to 35 large American blue-chip stocks, whose development correlated best with the Standard & Poor's stock index, and then took option contracts on them.

He claimed that he sold purchase rights (calls) on the index and bought selling rights (puts) on the index on an out-of-money basis. The selling rights, so he stated, were largely financed by selling purchase rights, and this was supposed to limit the risk for portfolio losses. Madoff himself kept

202 **SWINDLING BILLIONS**

his strategy as a "secret". The answer to those who dared to ask for details was that "it's a proprietary strategy" which he did not allow others to copy.

My suspicion is that few of the millionaire investors understood very much about sophisticated derivatives, including put and call options – it was not their field. They just trusted their great guru.

Some stock analysts and investment funds tried to back-test his investment strategy by using historical actual share prices for American stocks and index options. In these tests they were unable to replicate the profits he claimed.

When Madoff was questioned about this, he countered by arguing that "they did not do a good job". Strangely enough these negative tests did not create any stir.

Following Madoff's arrest the trustee appointed by the judicial authorities, the lawyer Irving Picard, stunned everybody with his announcement that Madoff had not in the past 13 years made any of the numerous security transactions that his strategy would have required. It was all illusory.

As Madoff never made any legitimate stock investments with his private clients' money, he probably deposited a good deal of these funds in his business account at the Chase Manhattan Bank. Chase and its successor JP Morgan Chase, according to the *Financial Times,* earned as much as $483 million from his bank account.

In the customary pyramid manner, most investors did not (until 2008) request any large payouts of their profits; they mainly enjoyed seeing their "paper profits" appearing on their accounts with Madoff. If investors actually requested cash withdrawals of their profits or capital from their accounts, those were financed with the fresh money flowing in from new investors and, to a limited extent, from interest payments on bank deposits. Certainly no money came in through the hyped investment strategy.

At one stage it was suspected (for instance, by Barron's) that Madoff was front running in his equity trading. This is an illegal practice by which a stock dealer buys shares for his own account if he has certain information that a client will come in with a large purchase order. When the client's purchase has raised the share price, the dealer can sell his own shares at a profit. But later on it was confirmed that he was certainly not front running – just purely swindling.

Suspicious Profits and Red Lights

The experienced American financial analyst and accountant, Harry Markopolos, had already filed a complaint about Madoff's business to the SEC in 1999, and asked them to investigate it. The title of Markopolos' lengthy memorandum was "The World's Largest Hedge Fund is a Fraud". It cited 29 problems.

His concluding remarks were: *"Bernie Madoff is running the world's largest unregistered hedge fund. He's organized this business as a hedge fund of funds… If this isn't a regulatory dodge, I don't know what is."* Markopolos' opinion was that it was either a Ponzi pyramid or front running. The ultimate conclusion was: probably a Ponzi.

Markopolos did a thorough analysis of Madoff's fund's improbably stable profits. He estimated that to be able to pay 12 per cent in annual profits to investors, Madoff had to earn 16 per cent gross continuously each year because he paid four per cent to feeder funds as a thank you for their "investment assistance". In his opinion, the figures just did not add up.

SEC investigated Madoff Securities at least eight times over 16 years. Some allegations were also made by a few financial experts other than Markopolos and by some whistleblowers. Yet, the SEC did not find anything suspicious.

The SEC also met with Markopolos in 2001 in order to discuss his claim that Madoff's firm used fraudulent methods. Even then nothing criminal was detected. As late as in 2007, an investment rule control team from the SEC investigated if Madoff had started a Ponzi scheme, but again nothing negative was found.

Critics contend, according to *USA Today*, that these investigations were incompetently handled. Even Madoff himself said to the *New York Daily News* that he could already have been caught in 2003, but bumbling investigators acted like "Lt. Colombo" and never asked the right questions.

The persistent and professional Markopolos struggled for almost ten years trying to unmask Madoff – but did not succeed until the market crisis unfolded, leaving Madoff in a hopeless liquidity squeeze. Due to Madoff's good relations with the SEC, nobody followed up on his allegations in-depth. Questioning Madoff seemed almost unthinkable.

In his testimony to Congress, according to Arvedlund, a bitter Markopolos argued that the SEC overlooked Madoff's fraud because the agency was "captive to the industry it regulates and it is afraid of bringing big cases against the largest, most powerful firms". In his opinion most SEC staffers suffered from "ineptitude and financial illiteracy". Markopolos published a book about his battle in 2010. It has an appropriate name, *No One Would Listen*.

Lavish Golf Club as Hunting Ground

The stylish golf and tennis club, Palm Beach Country Club, was one of Madoff's important working sites, located near his ostentatious seaside mansion. He had been introduced to this exclusive watering hole of the Eastern shore upper class by his New York and Florida contacts, as membership was not assured.

Besides being ultra-rich, its members were partly businessmen with a Jewish background. As a brother in faith, Madoff was on good terms with them. Many of them were smart-money types who knew the investment and business world very well. A nine-digit net wealth was nothing rare among the members.

The members played golf or tennis in the morning. Somebody insinuated that Madoff also cheated at golf, as he always seemed to have the same score. In the evening there was wining and dining, and frequently, charity functions.

The always smiling Madoff and his wife Ruth were known in the club as an unassuming couple. They never boasted about anything and fitted into a community where social climbers were not rare, even if they were despised.

Madoff succeeded in raising an estimated $1 billion in investments from the 330 club members. He probably received additional hundreds of millions, or even billions, from charities connected with them.

In general, Ponzi-style pyramids attract money from gullible common people. But now the targets were individuals who knew how to make money. They were fascinated by Madoff, partly because he never degraded himself by aggressive marketing.

In the Palm Beach Country Club, some newcomers with fat wallets happily paid the $350,000 membership entry fee only to get to know the investment guru personally and to invest in his miracle fund. Besides, the investments were not a pittance, but generally from a minimum of $5 million to $10 million up to $100 million.

In all likelihood, some of the shrewdest investors must have suspected that Madoff was cheating. But as in many other swindles, they dared to invest since they benefited from his cheating. He had been running his firm for so long that they felt he was a safe bet.

Besides, one of Madoff's trump cards was that he was well known for releasing investors' money instantly on request. In contrast, many other funds stipulated that investors must tie up their funds for a number of months, even years, like a long-term deposit, a "lock-up" in hedge fund vocabulary.

Negligent Millionaires and Investment Managers

The credulity of many large investors is surprising. Evidently most of them temporarily forgot the basic rule in the investment world: a careful analysis of the investment target, due diligence. And the old rule: "Trust, but verify."

None of the millionaire investors demanded a review of the firm's accounts by some well known accounting firm, such as one of the big four: Ernst & Young, Deloitte Touche Tohmatsu, KPMG or PricewaterhouseCoopers. The alarm bells should have rung because the firm's auditor was a tiny countryside firm with the name of Friehling & Horowitz.

It had only one active auditor, David C. Friehling. In 1993, he had already informed the American Institute of Certified Public Accountants (AICPA) that he no longer performed company audits. Only in 2007 did one hedge fund research and advisory firm, Aksia LLC, warn its clients against investing with Madoff's firm because its auditing company was so inadequately staffed. On top of everything, the Madoff firm's comptroller was happily based in Bermuda!

Investors neither questioned his investment strategy, nor the company's limited human and financial resources. They trusted the financial guru whom everybody knew, with whom they played and in whose company they dined. He was one of them. The investors moved in herds, following the example of other successful millionaires, their friends.

Another red flag was that Madoff's recorded profits were too continuous and constant. For instance, George Soros' Quantum Fund, which eventually grew to $20 billion, showed extremely profitable years with returns of up to 50 per cent. But they were followed by steep losses in bad years. It was volatile and the profits were unstable.

Madoff, on the other hand, claimed to have had only an amazing five down months since 1996. Charles Gradante of the Hennessee Group hedge fund research firm stated that "You can't go 10 to 15 years with only three or four down months. It's just impossible."

Investment funds naturally favour low volatility hedge funds because all investors hate losses. But Madoff's abnormally regular profits should have raised more questions.

Another suspicious sign was that although Madoff was a pioneer in electronic trading, he refused to provide his clients online access to their accounts. He sent out account statements only by mail, whereas most hedge funds email statements and allow them to be downloaded via computer for easier analysis by investors, and perhaps also securities experts – something which Madoff certainly wanted to avoid.

As Madoff refused to discuss any details of his investment strategy – which is quite understandable now, as it was entirely phoney – he did not accept any asset management professionals as clients. They could have rocked the boat.

With the benefit of hindsight, we see that Madoff's mammoth swindle also raises a lot of delicate questions concerning the moral responsibility of major asset managers. They are supposed to act as trustees of their investors. Madoff's over-generous fees and commissions evidently blinded so many European and American feeder funds that they shipped over their investors' billions to his fund without further research and due diligence.

For instance, one of the largest feeder funds was Access International founded by the French nobleman, René-Thierry Magon de la Villehuchet. It charged a 5 per cent (!) fee up front, an 0.8 per cent management fee and a 16 per cent performance fee for investments by clients into its Luxalpha SICAV-American Selection Fund. Its total investments in Madoff's fund were a staggering $1.4 billion.

A final red flag: interestingly enough none of the millionaires apparently complained that the bulk of their money was held in custody by Madoff's firm itself. As Arvedlund points out, there was no independent custodian, such as a bank. Instead, Madoff Securities had discretionary brokerage agreements and administered the assets freely, all in one package. A clear conflict of interests and a huge risk for the investor.

Banks as Intermediaries

Some European law firms engaged by major investors have, according to the *Financial Times,* started litigation in New York and Luxembourg at least against UBS and HSBC. It was believed that these banks acted as the largest European custodians for Madoff-related securities or funds, when some feeder funds channelled billions of dollars to Madoff's own fund.

In late 2010 the court-appointed trustee in the Madoff case, Irving Picard, also sued the prominent Swiss bank UBS and some other entities for more than $2 billion. UBS was accused of collaboration in Madoff's huge Ponzi scheme by sponsoring international feeder funds sending money to Madoff, thereby "lending an aura of legitimacy" to his activities.

Besides being aware of signs of improper activities in Madoff Securities, UBS "chose to enable Madoff's fraud for their own gain", said the trustee. He contended that "Madoff's scheme could not have been accomplished unless UBS had looked the other way". Defendants in the UBS case include people affiliated with Access International Advisers, and Luxalpha Sicav.

In early December 2010, Picard also sued the large HSBC bank for $9 billion. Seeking to recover funds on behalf of Madoff victims, he alleged 24 counts of fraud and misconduct against the bank as it aided Madoff's scheme through the creation of a network of international feeder funds. It followed a similar suit against JP Morgan Chase for $6 billion.

The complaint alleged that the defendants were well aware of the signs of fraud that were already circulating around Madoff's firm. "Had HSBC and the defendants reacted appropriately to such warnings and other obvious badges of fraud... the Madoff Ponzi scheme would have collapsed years, billions of dollars, and countless victims sooner", said Picard according to BBC Business News.

Purportedly, HSBC twice asked accountants KPMG to identify concerns regarding the Madoff firm, and KPMG twice reported serious risks already known to HSBC.

HSBC said it was defending itself "vigorously" against Madoff-related claims. It regarded the trustee's claims of wrongdoing unfounded.

Furthermore, Picard filed complaints on 9 December 2010 against seven other global financial institutions: Citigroup's Citibank, Natixis SA, Fortis, ABN Amro Bank, Banco Bilbao Vizcaya Argentaria, Nomura and Merrill Lynch, now owned by Bank of America.

Altogether, Picard had by 11 December 2010 filed some 30 lawsuits to try to recover perhaps $40 billion to $50 billion from banks and feeder funds that steered money to Madoff. The various defendants appeared to have made several hundred millions of dollars in fees from the scheme. By mid-December 2010, the trustee had recovered about $2.6 billion through settlements and asset sales.

However, 17 December 2010 was a good day for many Madoff victims, who had not had much cause for optimism. Kara Scannell of the *Financial Times* wrote that the estate of Jeffry Picower, a long-time Madoff investor found dead in his Florida pool in 2009, had agreed to hand the enormous sum of nearly $7.2 billion to the victims in the largest recovery since the fraud came to light in 2008. The agreement with federal prosecutors and Irving Picard was approved by a federal judge in the biggest forfeiture in the history of the US Department of Justice.

The agreement bolstered the recovery of Madoff funds to almost $9.8 billion. Picower had started investing with Madoff in the 1970s, and the Picower accounts deposited $619 million and got "astronomical" triple-digit rates of return. As he withdrew $7.8 billion before the crash, the net withdrawal was almost $7.2 billion. His wife, who according to the trustee had shown helpfulness and good faith in the negotiations, said her husband "was in no way complicit in Madoff's fraud". Recovered funds will start to be distributed to qualified victims in 2011.

Some Madoff investors started to work with so-called distressed debt investors to put the affair behind them. In 2010, many victims had received solicitations from various funds offering up to 31 cents on the dollar for selling their Madoff claims. Including the mentioned large recovery deal, one of the distressed debt investors said the estate was much closer to recovering 50 per cent of their claims, wrote Dam McCrum and Anousha Sakoui of the *Financial Times*.

A final spectacular attack against some banks and feeder funds suspected of having been mixed up in the sad Madoff affair was launched by Irving Picard on 10 December 2010. He filed a whopping $19.6 billion lawsuit accusing almost 60 people and institutions, including Italy's and Austria's largest banks, of having participated in a decade-long "illegal scheme". He was seeking the return of investors' funds and bank fees, plus damages.

The suit, the largest and most serious civil claim filed in this connection, targeted Bank Medici, the failed Austrian bank, its former president Sonja Kohn, Bank Austria and UniCredit, partial owners of Bank Medici, for allegedly having participated in a "conspiracy" funnelling the appalling sum of $9.1 billion to Madoff, wrote Brooke Masters of the *Financial Times*.

The trustee's complaint against Bank Medici, discussed later in the book, marked the first time he had filed a civil "racketeering" suit, a particularly serious claim allowing him to seek triple damages. In his opinion, Kohn "had masterminded a vast illegal scheme... not only to support the Madoff fraud, but also to enrich herself, her family and the largest banks in Austria and Italy".

Kohn was allegedly at the centre of a 23-year conspiracy, netting her a total of at least $62 million in "kickbacks". Picard maintained that:

"In Sonja Kohn, Madoff found a criminal soulmate, whose greed and dishonest inventiveness equalled his own."

The lawsuit also alleged that Kohn had already worked out a deal with Madoff in 1987. She would be paid a flat fee for bringing clients to his operation. Before confessing, Madoff supposedly destroyed the secret records about his dealings with Kohn, but former employees kept copies.

She apparently recruited her first Madoff client in 1989, a Chicago business contact of her husband.

The Medici Bank essentially worked as a branch of the large Bank Austria, which owned 25 per cent of it, managing its accounts and portfolios and providing staff on a rotating basis. The lawsuit claimed that it had received $31 million in fees from Medici. Over the years Kohn's businesses opened outposts in Italy, Germany, Gibraltar and the Cayman Islands.

UniCredit is a pillar of the Italian economy, with over $1,300 billion in assets and a presence in 22 countries. It is also one of Europe's largest banks. UniCredit bought Bank Austria in 2005. The $19.6-billion lawsuit named UniCredit's former chief executive, Alessandro Profumo, alongside more than 50 defendants, including UniCredit's asset management arm, Pioneer, according to Rachel Sanderson of the *Financial Times*. Profumo left UniCredit on 20 September 2010, having received an overwhelming vote of no-confidence from his board after 15 years as chief executive.

A lawyer for the former Bank Medici and Kohn said they would fight the "completely wrong allegations". Also, the UniCredit bank said it would defend itself "vigorously". None of the defendants in the trustee's lawsuit was criminally charged.

Most of the large number of banks sued by Picard before this action also said they would fight the claims. However, one of the alleged large losers in the Madoff swindle, Union Bancaire Privée, reportedly agreed to pay up to $500 million to settle the allegations.

The reason for suing so many institutions in late 2010 was that the time limit for making complaints in the Madoff case ended on 11 December 2010, two years after the arrest of Bernard Madoff.

The French asset management group for private individuals, Meeschaert Gestion Privé, decided to pay damages to its "Madoffed" clients. On behalf of many clients, Meeschaert had made investments in the above-mentioned Luxalpha fund located in Luxembourg, which, in its turn, channelled the money over into Madoff's fund.

This was the first French case in which investors were compensated for their Madoff-related losses. Meeschaert decided to go ahead with this to maintain its clients' trust. It repaid the full capital investment sum to its clients, but not the nominal profits, which even according to the authorities were fictive.

An astounding 720,000 investors outside the US who lost money to Madoff have settled with their banks, receiving $15.5 billion in all, according to law firms acting for global victims of the fraud, wrote financial journalists Minder and Henriques. Many were Spanish and Latin American investors. The compensation covered the invested capital, but not the sham profits. Banco Santander, one of the largest banks in the world, alone settled €2.33 billion, being the third most important Madoff casualty worldwide.

The National Bank of Kuwait returned $50 million to about 20 rich investors. Reportedly the large sovereign wealth fund, Abu Dhabi Investment Authority, also indirectly invested $400 million with Madoff.

Not all banks and major investors fell into Madoff's trap. For example, Goldman Sachs and Crédit Suisse informed their large clients that the Madoff fund was not on their approved list of intermediaries.

The reason for Goldman's cold attitude towards Madoff, according to Arvedlund, may have been the following: although Madoff's investment strategy would have required massive trading in stock options and derivatives, none of the professionals in the field had heard about or seen these big trades happening. Neither the trading pit in Chicago nor the head of Goldman's trading desk had heard of him. As Goldman would not trade with Madoff's firm, that was one kiss of death.

Crédit Suisse urged its clients to withdraw their money from the Madoff firm because they could not determine how he made money. Perhaps Madoff's exceptionally high commissions to all and sundry who delivered new investors to him may have been seen as an alarming sign.

As early as 2003, the big French bank, Société Générale, sent a letter to its investment clients, in which it recommended that they stay clear of Madoff's fund.

There were also attempts to lure the billionaire Donald Trump into the Madoff fund. But Trump declined the offers, although Madoff had joined the golf club which bears Trump's name.

Madoff's Mystery

Bernie Madoff was and still is an enigma, even in his lonely jail cell in North Carolina. How did he really succeed in defrauding so many mega-rich people and charities in the United States and abroad? Why did the victims not check the basic facts, starting from the quality of the audit? Why did they trust him so blindly?

Nobody will perhaps ever know exactly how and when the Wall Street legend started his fraudulent activities in New York, Palm Beach, Hollywood and elsewhere. At the latest it must have started around the mid-1990s.

From year to year the client list just grew longer and longer, with increasingly more celebrities and other moneyed people. They found it irresistible to refuse the discreet market guru's services, reserved only for selected individuals, and promising seemingly safe annual profits – especially since so many other established businessmen and millionaires had been trailblazers.

Madoff's almost lifelong family friend, textile billionaire Carl Shapiro, was of great help to him. Shapiro enjoyed much respect in Palm Beach, and his backing further propped up Madoff's reputation.

Shapiro had got to know Madoff in the early 1960s. He admired the young former lifesaver and broker-dealer who had invested his first dollars in stocks. The friendly Shapiro helped Madoff on the way by entrusting him with $100,000 (over $700,000 today) to invest.

The two men's friendship continued for almost 50 years. Madoff became the son whom Shapiro did not have. He was invited to all of the Shapiro family's celebrations, weddings and birthdays. Madoff became the trustee handling the Shapiro clan's investments.

When the already 95-year-old Shapiro learnt about Madoff's arrest in December 2008, he confessed in an interview published by the *Palm Beach Daily News* that it "felt like a dagger straight into my heart".

The philanthropist and large-scale donator is estimated to have lost the enormous sum of $545 million in the Madoff debacle. That also included the $250 million that he threw in at the last moment, having received Madoff's emergency call for help when he was trying to save himself from bankruptcy in late 2008.

On top of that, in December 2010 the family of Carl Shapiro struck a deal with the trustee and prosecutors, agreeing to repay $625 million of profits that Shapiro had received from Madoff earlier on.

The Huge Losses of Wealthy Americans

Some rich Hollywood film directors and stars, who had accumulated millions of dollars, were easy prey for the great financial shark. One of them was Steven Spielberg, one of the world's most influential film personalities and directors, awarded with many Oscars. His blockbuster movies include *Jaws, E.T. the Extra-Terrestrial, Indiana Jones, Saving Private Ryan* and *Schindler's List.*

Spielberg's colleague, Jeffrey Katzenberg, also grieved over his losses. He is CEO of Dreamworks, which they put up together, and director of Walt Disney, as well as producer of the *Shrek* animations.

Among the film stars who forfeited millions was Zsa Zsa Gabor, happily married eight times. She was reportedly "very, very angry". The same Gabor who once philosophised that she'd rather cry on the backseat of a Rolls Royce than a Volkswagen.

Another victim suffering horrific losses was popular film star John Malkovich, leading actor in many box-office record films, such as *Empire of the Sun, In the Line of Fire, Being John Malkovich* and *Dangerous Liaisons.*

Screenwriter Eric Roth, of *Forrest Gump* fame, was also one of the unlucky investors. He is said to have lost a good deal of his savings.

Recent estimates suggest that, excluding the countless indirect non-US victims mentioned earlier, there were altogether 13,500 individual Madoff account victims. Among those was the former model, Carmen Dell'Orifice, from New York City.

Dell'Orifice was a friend of real estate millionaire Norman F. Levy, who enjoyed his retirement, travelled wide and far and donated to charities. He also "invested positively" into socially responsible companies and projects, with the help of his good friend Bernie Madoff.

Madoff was happy to socialise with people who were as rich as he himself. "Small people" did not interest him at all.

According to the revelations of journalist Mark Seal of *Vanity Fair* magazine, Levy had already set up a meeting between Dell'Orifice and Madoff in 1994, in his head office in New York. Without her knowing it, Levy transferred $100,000 to her bank account, and he impressed on her that it was a rare honour to be allowed to invest money in Madoff's exclusive fund.

Dell'Orifice became Madoff's friend. Her initial investment, including some major additional capital infusions and steady profits, eventually grew into millions. Levy was delighted with Dell'Orifice's pecuniary success. Time and again he sung Madoff's praises in tones such as "Madoff is my son", meaning he was his surrogate son and, therefore, a member of his own family.

Madoff enjoyed the company of Levy, who was 26 years his senior, and thanked him as "a mentor and a patron for 40 years". After the catastrophe, Dell'Orifice mused about Levy's constant superlatives such as "Bernie is the most respectable and intelligent person". That attested to Madoff's phenomenal ability to deceive even intelligent people who had experienced almost everything.

He stole from his friends and victims with a smile on his face. Madoff's family friend, Dell'Orifice, lost all her life's savings.

When Levy died in 2005 at the age of 93, Madoff had delivered a commemorative speech at the funeral. His estate was left with $244 million, part of which was donated to a cancer charity. Both Levy's children had already received their share of the inheritance earlier and had established their own charities. Acting as the trustee of the family, Madoff had taken care of the charities' investments, with the result that they had to be closed in December 2008, having lost all their money.

Another rich businessman cum victim lost $50 million overnight. He moaned to Mark Seal: "My charity was wiped out, my foundation was wiped out, the retirement for my employees was wiped out."

Others compared the events to the Titanic disaster: when people learnt about their giant losses, they started screaming and yelling in their despair.

> "Bernie stole even our confidence," said a long-time
> colleague who parted with most of his savings.

Following the catastrophe, some of the Palm Beach Country Club members were reportedly forced to sell their Florida houses and yachts. At the same time, they probably left the club with sad memories.

Charities Also Fleeced

Private charities play a very important role in the United States. The 72,000 charities donate billions of dollars to their favourite causes in normal years. Their wealth is partly due to the tax exemption on donations.

The charities have generally invested their assets in a cautious, risk-averse manner, as a minimum to conserve their capital. Perhaps they regarded Madoff's fund as a safe bet. But now many of them have lost altogether billions of dollars collected with great effort.

Among the unfortunate ones were charities supporting cancer victims, Alzheimer patients, autistic children, battered wives and diabetics, never mind charities that helped universities, students, museums, orchestras and young artists. Some, including the Chais Family Foundation, the Robert I. Lappin Charitable Foundation, the Picower Foundation and the JEHT Foundation, even had to close their doors, having lost their money.

One of the prominent losers was Nobel Peace Prize winner and Holocaust survivor Eliel Wieser. His charity lost $15.2 million, and most of his own and his wife's life savings went up in smoke.

Wiesel said in February 2009 that he was no financial genius, but that he had verified with "the best brains on Wall Street" that it was safe to invest in Madoff's fund. "We thought he was God," Wiesel said in a conference speech. "We entrusted everything in his hands." Now Wiesel brands Madoff "a thief, a scoundrel and a criminal".

Madoff's swindle has wide repercussions on the American society, as the slashed grants from many charities affect the lives of hundreds of thousands of citizens, perhaps even millions. Even the International Olympic Committee was among those swindled.

As Madoff looted so many charities, it is interesting to note that his own favourite charity, the Lymphoma Research Foundation, to which he had donated about $6 million, did not invest in his fund. His son Andrew had been diagnosed with lymphoma. The private Madoff Family Foundation's assets of $19 million were frozen by the court.

European Millionaires "Madoffed"

After Madoff's arrest it was estimated that dozens of hedge funds and feeder funds held a total of $20 billion or more with Madoff. They included the Union Bancaire Privée (UBP) based in Geneva, which lost about $700 million. Madoff was one of UBP's top five holdings.

Besides the Spanish Banco Santander, another loser was Pioneer Alternative Investments, part of the Italian bank UniCredit. Interestingly enough, Banco Santander paid $235 million to the Madoff victims' trust.

One of the first large private victims in Europe was the principal owner of the worldwide cosmetics firm L'Oréal, the 86-year-old Liliane Bettencourt. *Le Figaro* magazine revealed that her original Madoff investment through the Luxalpha fund in Luxembourg was $400 million to $500 million. However, the intelligent lady smelled a rat and cashed in most of her investment – only a paltry $50 million went down the drain.

Other European investors hit by the Madoff scam were reportedly Britain's Merseyside and Hampshire pension funds, Deutsche Bank Italia pension funds, Danish and Dutch retirement giant PFA Pension and the Shell pension fund. Switzerland's St. Gallen Kantonalbank also lost money.

The global HSBC bank had lent a hair-raising $1 billion to investors who could use their Madoff fund investments as collateral for the loans, according to Erin Arvedlund.

Another great "very very angry" loser was the renowned fashion designer, Daniel Hechter. He has been called the inventor of ready-made clothes. Hechter lost most of his assets as a result of Madoff's deceit.

The world-famous film director, Pedro Almodóvar, was also reportedly "Madoffed". Some of his films seen by hundreds of millions of movie goers are *All About My Mother, Talk To Her, Bad Education* and *Return.*

Affinity Theft and the "Swindler's List"

Rabbi Mark Borowitz's Los Angeles charity lost at least $200,000 in Madoff's affinity theft. Madoff exploited the unyielding belief that you always can trust your own people. Borowitz commented to Mark Seal:

"Whether it's Latino or black or Jewish or Christian, everybody wants to trust their own. Bernie Madoff took our trust and raped it... He took advantage of every vulnerability, because he knew our vulnerable spots."

The Los Angeles *Jewish Journal* published an article about the thousands of victims, many of them Jewish. It called the list of victims collected by the official trustee, Irving Picard, the *Swindler's List*.

The name alluded to *Schindler's List*, a 1993 American epic film about Oscar Schindler and persecuted Jews. Schindler was a German businessman who saved the lives of more than one thousand Polish-Jewish refugees during the Holocaust by employing them in his factories in Poland.

By coincidence, the film was directed by Steven Spielberg, himself one of Madoff's victims figuring in the Swindler's List.

Secure Investment?

Madoff defrauded his billions from people who knew how to make money. Curiously enough, most victims saw his fund as a conservative money market investment, backed by solid US government treasury bills – like a "Steady-Eddie" fund.

Some of Madoff's clients played the spread, a very dangerous game. One example: somebody who in the early 2000s owned a mortgage-free $15-million house in Florida could easily obtain a mortgage loan on it of $10 million from the bank, at 4 per cent interest. The interest cost was $400,000 a year.

If the borrower then invested his $10-million loan money from the bank into Madoff's fund at a 10 per cent annual profit after taxes, the 6 percentage point difference between the carrying costs for the loan and the return on the investment yielded the house owner $600,000 in annual profit.

The seed for the catastrophe had been planted: the Madoff investment was wiped out at the end of 2008 and house prices collapsed. When the bank called the loan and the borrower did not have the $10 million to repay it, the bank foreclosed the house and sold it cheaply on the weak housing market – often at an outrageous discount.

Suddenly, such a derring-do investor found himself both penniless and homeless.

What Happened to the Money?

The exact amount of money lost by the victims will never be known. Picard put the investors' losses at $18 billion. Other current estimates vary between $12 billion and $20 billion.

Picard's chief counsel, David Sheehan, said in September 2009 that $36 billion was invested into the scam, $18 billion returned to investors, and $18 billion missing. About half of Madoff's investors were allegedly "net winners", earning more than they had invested.

The money withdrawn in the final six years is subject to "claw back" (return of money) law suits.

The reason for the incredibly much lower loss estimates than the $65 billion mentioned earlier on is that much of the vanished money never existed in reality, except in Madoff's phoney profit statements to clients. He actually never viewed his clients' profits as real, only as "paper profits".

Over the years, Madoff also spent a good deal of the money invested on paying out capital and profits to those who requested them. Roughly $12 billion was "rescued" through the capital restitutions demanded by panicking clients in 2008, especially during the acute stock market crisis in autumn. Madoff also lent money to his loss-making brokerage firm.

Additionally, he also used his company as a personal piggy bank. The firm and he himself were one and the same. His family lived a life of luxury paid for by other people's money. One sign of the easy-money culture was that an amazing $173 million in signed cheques were found in Madoff's office desk after his arrest, probably intended for bonuses to the family and some non-family employees.

He favoured his own family members within the firm. Most members of the larger family were on his payroll. His own people were safe choices and completely under his control.

Wife Ruth Madoff was in charge of the firm's bank accounts. Younger brother Peter acted as senior managing director and chief compliance officer. Peter's daughter, Shana, was a lawyer and compliance attorney. Even Peter's wife, Marion, earned $163,500 in 2008, according to the *International Herald Tribune*, although there is no evidence that she actually worked in the firm.

Madoff's two sons, Mark and Andrew, worked as stock traders, as did his nephew, Charles Weiner. Andrew reportedly invested a fair deal of money in his father's fund, while Mark was not an investor in the firm. The reasons for this may perhaps gradually become clear.

Besides family members, there were others on the payroll of Bernard L. Madoff Investment Securities who did not work within the firm, such as boat captains, housekeepers and other helpers. Madoff owned a luxury yacht and a $24-million Embraer Legacy private jet jointly with his good friend, real estate tycoon Eddie Blumenfeld. It was painted with the BM logo. This friend also suffered heavy losses in Madoff's crash.

His splendid homes in Florida, Long Island, France and Manhattan were apparently not used much for promoting the firm's business.

Madoff's leisure time activities were costly. He paid $471,000 dollars to the Long Island Marina. Membership fees to exclusive clubs swallowed almost $1 million a year, including the Breakers in Palm Beach, Atlantic City Country Club on Long Island, Palm Beach Country Club and Trump International Golf Club.

According to a 13 March 2009 filing by Madoff, he and his wife were worth up to $126 million, plus an estimated $700 million for the value of his business interest in Bernard Madoff Investment Securities.

Their other major assets included securities of $45 million, cash of $17 million, a half-interest in the BLM Air Charter of $12 million, a Leopard yacht worth $7 million, $2.6 million of jewellery, a Manhattan apartment worth $7 million, a Montauk home worth $3 million, a Palm Beach home worth $11 million, a Cap d'Antibes property worth $1 million and $9.9 million worth of furniture, household goods and art.

The houses and boats were auctioned by the US Marshals Service in late 2009. In addition, the Service organised several other auctions in New York in 2010 (and one was planned in Florida for spring 2011), covering thousands of personal and household items. They included many watches and jewellery, among other things, a 10.5-carat diamond engagement ring, kitchen utensils, shoes, furniture and beds, books and a grand Steinway & Sons piano used for decoration. Even his fancy pleated boxer shorts were on sale, reported Thomas Kaplan.

A pair of slippers bearing Madoff's initials in gold thread ranked among the top attractions. The proceeds of these household sales amounting to several million dollars went to the victims of the fraud.

On his frequent trips to London, Madoff stayed at the Lanesborough Hotel, one of the most expensive in the world. Guests pay up to £8,000 per night for a spacious suite and have their own private on-call butler. Madoff left a trunk of clothes at the Lanesborough, which the hotel stored, cleaned, pressed and hung in his suite for the next visit, according to Arvedlund.

Mark Madoff owed his parents $22 million; and Andrew Madoff $9.5 million. The firm lent almost $11 million to the two of them for the purchase of homes, but the investigators found no sign of any loan repayments. The brother, Peter, benefited from a $7 million loan in 2007.

$2.7 million in company money was allegedly used to buy a house in New Jersey for a long-time employee, JoAnn Crup. She was arrested in November 2010 together with Annette Bongiorno, head of the (Ponzi) advisory unit. Reportedly, the two ladies had been in charge of the fake accounts.

The Wife's Role

Having started to work in 1960 in the Bernard L. Madoff Investment Securities firm, Ruth Madoff checked, besides the firm's accounts, all incoming bills and made all related payments.

As Ruth's father, Saul Alpern played a decisive role in recruiting rich investors to Madoff's fund, some people suspected that he was the mastermind behind Madoff's original fund-raising template. Since Ruth had worked in the firm for so long, she obviously knew the investment field reasonably well. According to Mark Seal, Madoff once commented to his secretary: "I've always had Ruth watching the books. *Nothing* gets by Ruth."

For these reasons, questions were raised about Ruth Madoff's possible role in the swindle. Why did she rush into her husband's office just one day before his arrest to draw $10 million from their private account? Apparently she suspected that the arrest was coming. Somewhat earlier, Madoff had transferred $7 million to companies owned by his wife, sons and niece.

Did the wife know about the long-lasting fraud, and if so, how much did she know? Did Bernie Madoff take all the blame on his shoulders in order to save his own family, his brother and his relatives?

In any case, if the wife was not aware of the huge swindle, which was such a heavy blow to her sons, her behaviour after the disclosure seemed strange. A natural reaction would have been to leave the world-record swindler who had cheated and disgraced her, and to start comforting the couple's sons, who were completely devastated.

Even her son Mark's wife, Stephanie, applied in 2010 to have the last name of her and her children changed to "Morgan", citing threats to the family. But Ruth Madoff stood faithfully by her husband's side. She allegedly fought tooth and nail to keep over $60 million of the family's riches, which according to the government investigators, did not belong to her. In the summer of 2009, she came to an agreement with the prosecutor that she could keep only $2.5 million dollars in assets, while the rest of the couple's enormous property was transferred to the American authorities. No charges have been brought against her.

Even Ruth Madoff's sister, Joan, who lived in Florida, lost $2.7 million. To add insult to injury, her husband forfeited $8.7 million. In fact, both sisters had placed money they had inherited from their parents into Madoff's fund.

The luxurious life of the great swindler's wife suffered a heavy blow. Two small examples from everyday life: her favourite hairdresser refused to bleach Ruth Madoff's hair, and her trusted florist closed the door in the face of her former long-time customer.

The US Internal Revenue Winner

As an irony of fate, one of the winners from Madoff's swindle may be the US tax authority, the Internal Revenue Service (IRS). Over the years it had apparently been able to collect at least hundreds of millions of dollars in capital gains taxes on the enormous phantom profits from Madoff's fund.

The Madoff victims' biggest disagreement with the government was exactly this, that normal capital gains taxes had been duly paid on what turned out to be completely fake paper profits, which many victims had absolutely not seen anywhere other than on their bogus account statements, let alone cashed in.

In addition, the Treasury department investigators have discovered that quite a few Madoff investors funnelled their money to offshore accounts, without reporting them in their tax returns. Therefore, in March 2009 the US authorities claimed a number of billion dollars in compensation for tax debts which had arisen during several decades. By March 2009 about $1 billion of such tax debts had been collected.

In addition, the IRS will probably be able to level severe penalties on these tax dodgers for hiding money offshore.

Bank Medici Great Loser

One of the great losers was Bank Medici, which played a key role in the expansion of Madoff's business in Europe and also in Russia, and was sued in December 2010, as stated earlier.

Despite its impressive name, this Austrian bank had nothing to do with the Medicis, the most powerful business family in Florence between the 1200s and 1700s. The Medici family ran a majestic financial and political establishment known all over Europe during the Renaissance.

The new bank with the imaginative name was founded only in 1994 in Vienna by the above-mentioned Sonja Kohn, who owned 75 per cent of it. Bank Austria Creditanstalt, the country's largest bank, and the Italian financial conglomerate, UniCredit Group, were listed as minority shareholders. The relationship with Bank Austria added greatly to Kohn's credibility.

Bank Medici got a full banking licence from the Austrian financial authority in 2003. Its business was brisk and it had good relations with other banks marketing Medici's funds to rich private investors above all in Europe and especially Russia. Many investors who bought shares in the Medici funds were evidently not aware that one important final destination was actually a certain Madoff fund.

According to financial reporter Erin Arvedlund, Bank Medici won prizes in Europe for "amazing" performance still in November 2008. Its flagship Herald USA Fund, started in 1996, reported a return of 6.5 per cent for the year through 28 November 2008, with assets of more than

$1.9 billion. Competitors could not match that. Most of them had lost an average of 17 per cent as the global credit crisis bit into returns.

Originally, it was alleged that Bank Medici funnelled about $3.2 billion into Madoff investments, but official estimates by the trustee Picard later ran as high as $9.1 billion. For these exceptional services, the bank received generous fees and commissions from Madoff.

Following Madoff's arrest, US bank regulators found records suggesting that Bank Medici had pocketed many millions of dollars a year for bringing in new money to Madoff through Cohmad Securities. Sonja Kohn and Medici were definitely believed to be among Madoff's most important feeder funds in Europe.

It was also suspected that Sonja Kohn got doubly paid, firstly in the form of kickbacks from Madoff himself, but secondly also in fees from investors whose cash was paid into Medici's feeder funds and further channelled to Madoff. Kohn allegedly characterised herself as "the gateway to Madoff".

A substantial portion of Medici's investments came from billionaire Russian oligarchs. As Kohn, the bank's principal owner, suddenly disappeared from the spotlight into hiding, it was rumoured that she feared grim revenge from her angry Moscow "comrades".

The bank's licence was revoked and it is now under Austrian state supervision under a new name, 20.20 Medici AG. A group of Bank Medici's clients from Israel, Russia and the Ukraine filed a complaint in Vienna's criminal court, accusing the bank and Kohn of fraud and breach of trust.

Fairfield Greenwich Group as Main Feeder Fund

The Manhattan-located investment fund, Fairfield Greenwich Group, was also one of the main Madoff suppliers. It employed 140 persons in 2008 and its asset management portfolio counted an impressive $14.1 billion.

The Fairfield Greenwich Group sold its investment services actively and took pride in its good relations with Madoff. Besides delivering huge amounts of money from wealthy Americans, it passed on billions to him from seriously rich international investors, especially from Europe and South America.

Fairfield Greenwich apparently appealed to Madoff for one basic reason: its investment capital came from completely different sources than his customary ones. Madoff himself operated mainly within the United States' North-Eastern Jewish circles, while Fairfield and its CEO, Walter Noel, worked with Christian circles and had close business relations in the Waspy Greenwich, Connecticut, where he lived.

Noel, with his Harvard degree, was important for Madoff because he was an outside third-party "aristocratic" personality who blessed Madoff's business and gave it increased credibility, says Arvedlund.

As a result, an unusually high proportion, about half of Fairfield's total investments, was directed into Madoff's fund. Earlier on, in 2004, Fairfield's focus on Madoff had been almost outrageous, as a whopping 85 per cent of its assets had been invested with Madoff.

In the asset management field, such excessive reliance on one single fund represented a completely unique accumulation of investment risk. It was by no means in harmony with a fund of funds policy, whose main idea is to disperse its risks in different types of assets.

Curiously enough Fairfield had presented itself as a cautious, low-risk investment fund. In its brochures it bragged about its considerably more in-depth due diligence analyses than the competition. The gimmicky slogans about Fairfield's risk-averse investment policy were probably all eyewash.

In all likelihood, the reason for Fairfield Greenwich's heavily Madoff-oriented investment strategy was that he did not charge them any asset management fees whatsoever. On the contrary, he paid them a few per cent in kickbacks for the investment assistance. Normally, investment fund managers such as Madoff would annually take two per cent on the capital and 20 per cent of all profits they made for their clients. However, Madoff's main objective was to secure a continuous large net inflow of capital to his fund.

Consequently, investing with Madoff meant that Fairfield saved a great deal on costs and got a good bonus, at the same time as it probably charged its own clients one per cent on the capital and 20 per cent on the profits. On top of that, feeder funds such as Fairfield charged various trading fees. It was all highly lucrative for Fairfield.

Losing such a significant part of their investment portfolios overnight was a terrible blow to Fairfield's asset management clients. Both the state of Massachusetts and the estate trustee have alleged that victims are owed money from feeder funds such as Fairfield.

After Madoff's arrest, Fairfield staff worked furiously to provide evidence of the due diligence they had never actually done. One outside banker even confided to Arvedlund: "They're playing stupid right now, playing the victim. They full well knew of multiple questions about Madoff's operation, reporting, accounting."

Madoff's confession killed off many of his feeder funds. Fairfield Greenwich Group continued to keep its doors open, but dismissed most of its staff.

Absolute Return magazine noted that the top feeder funds that closed included Fairfield Sentry Fund, which lost an estimated $6.9 billion, and the Gabriel Capital Group and Ascot Partners, which forfeited $3.3 billion in assets connected with Madoff. Tremont Group's Rye family of funds lost $3.1 billion and Kingate Management $2.7 billion.

How Could Madoff Have Continued for So Long?

As Madoff's fund did not do any real equity investments on behalf of its clients for at least 13 years, it was amazing that the fraud could continue for such a long time. He made an incredible number of untruthful declarations and sent falsified accounting and other reports to the SEC.

Madoff also mailed monthly phoney investment portfolio account statements to his many thousands of clients. These reports could not have been based on random figures because many investors knew the capital markets quite well. Besides, they also relied on other securities professionals. Therefore, the reports had to look absolutely genuine.

If Madoff alone, as he claimed in court, had prepared all these falsified monthly reports, he would have been the busiest guy of his own generation. But more than half a year after his arrest, his long-time key lieutenant and finance chief, Frank DiPascali, confessed that he had abetted Madoff in all these activities.

DiPascali pleaded guilty to securities fraud, money laundering and other charges that carry potential penalties of up to 125 years in prison. He was released on a $10-million bail in early 2010 and agreed to cooperate with the prosecutors and reveal all the fraudulent methods used, and also to assist the court in other ways.

DiPascali has provided important information leading to the arrests of the two important computer programmers mentioned below, Madoff's longtime auditor and the two back office ladies. DiPascali's cooperation has delayed his sentencing on his guilty plea. He and his wife have given up practically all their assets, estimated to be worth more than $6 million, to the government.

Two computer programmers who worked for Madoff's firm were arrested in their homes in November 2009. They were accused by the US attorney's office in Manhattan of helping to cover up his giant fraud scheme. They are Jerome O'Hara, 46, and George Perez, 43.

The two men are accused of providing the technical support needed to produce all false documents and trading records that were used to defraud investors. The SEC also separately filed a civil complaint against the two men, claiming that "without the help of O'Hara and Perez, the Madoff fraud would not have been possible. They used their special computer skills to create sophisticated, credible and entirely phoney trading records that were critical to the success of Madoff's scheme for so many years".

When the programmers at one stage had second thoughts about their illicit activities, perhaps even refusing to lie any longer, Madoff had instructed DiPascali to pay them "whatever they wanted in order to keep them happy", according to Diana Henriques of the *International Herald Tribune*.

Madoff shed some light on how he could continue for so long in a later jailhouse interview with the SEC's inspector general, David Kotz, who was charged with investigating how SEC had handled (and mishandled) the Madoff supervision over the years. Madoff said the young investigators who pestered him over small incidentals such as email messages should have just checked the basics, like his account with Wall Street's clearing house and his dealings with the firms that were supposedly handling his trades.

"If you're looking at a Ponzi scheme, it's the first thing you do," said Madoff, according to Henriques. Despite the SEC's "cronic ineptitude" Madoff was actually already sure in 2003–2004 and then again in 2006 that he would be caught, but the SEC once again botched the investigations.

Why Did Madoff Become A Criminal?

Bernard Madoff did not need to be a swindler. In 1986, the *Financial World* magazine already included Madoff on the list of the top 100 highest paid people on Wall Street, with estimated earnings of $6 million ($12 million today). He built up his firm to become one of the largest securities traders on Wall Street.

As an astute businessman and financial guru, he was successful, powerful and rich.

Why did he build a fictive, fraudulent world around him, when the real honest world had already given him so much? Why did he choose a road that led to a dead end, which swept him into disgrace and jailed him for the rest of his life? An end result that he confessed to having anticipated in March 2009.

One theory is that Madoff had failed in some large stock trading operations, and that he tried to cover the monumental losses by resorting to a sophisticated Ponzi.

Another possibility is that Madoff, coming from modest surroundings and seeing all the millionaires around him in his early life, decided that one day he would catch up, one day he would show them. His early success may have seduced him to acquire ever more: luxurious homes in attractive locations, yachts, planes, the millionaire club life, wealth for his family members, rich friends, all of it – not slowly but now, now, now.

Eleanor Squillari, Madoff's secretary, once asked him what he thought about the $6-million loss that his friend, Noel Levine, incurred because his secretary had embezzled such a large sum from him.

Madoff thought aloud: "Well, you know what happens is, it starts out with you taking a little bit, maybe a few hundred, a few thousand. You get comfortable with that, and before you know it, it snowballs into something big."

The real estate firm owner, Levine, who shared office space with Madoff's firm, suffered further two-digit million losses in the Madoff swindle. The 80-year-old gentleman was petrified by the new calamity.

How can it humanly be explained that Madoff's closest family friends were in the top tier among the victims? Friends and mentors who, in the course of many decades, had done everything to promote his rise to fame and riches.

The same question concerns his closest colleagues, from whom he stole their life savings. What kind of conscience does a man have, who on top of everything, robbed hundreds of charities?

One theory is that Madoff's advisory business was actually his own expensive way of borrowing money from the wealthy public, says Erin Arvedlund. There may be something to this, since at one stage Madoff's credit requests had been rejected by several banks in the United States and Europe.

Through his "advisory" fund he was able to raise capital for his legal broker-dealer business. At the same time he avoided the detailed due diligence of his company that would be a precondition for any bank to grant such large corporate loans. He wanted the cover of secrecy and may have thought that "paying" a mostly fictive 10 to 15 per cent a year to his advisory clients was a cheap "rate of interest".

Another possibility is that as the SEC closed down two of Madoff's early largest fund raisers, Frank Avellino and Michael Bienes, in 1992, it was the last straw which tipped the advisory operation over to a full Ponzi.

Greed Overtaken by Fear

The 1990s and early 2000s were wild decades in the global stock markets. It was the perfect environment for Madoff to pursue his billion-dollar swindle.

But as the stock markets collapsed in 2008 during the worst financial crisis for eight decades, Madoff's house of cards tottered. Investors' greed was overtaken by panic, by a veritable stampede.

Some major investors panicked and started to cash in their gigantic investments in Madoff Investment Securities. About $7 billion was called and withdrawn in the autumn of 2008, on top of the $5 billion that had already been cashed in earlier in the year. Madoff faced a deadlock, a hopeless liquidity squeeze.

One can, of course, speculate if Madoff would have been able to continue his swindling construction until the end of his days since he was already 70 years old. Evidently he personally thought that it would have succeeded, in the absence of the violent stock market and banking crisis.

To prop up his company's cash position, Madoff could in December

2008 still collect the $250-million loan from his old friend, Carl J. Shapiro, the 95-year-old philanthropist and businessman from Boston who tried to help him avoid bankruptcy. That was not nearly enough. In the weeks before his arrest he desperately tried to raise more funds from other friends, without success. The game was up.

On 10 December, 2008 Madoff proposed to his sons, Mark and Andrew, that the company should pay an astounding $173 million in bonuses two months in advance. Apparently the two boys were not aware of the firm's imminent collapse and pressed their father for an answer: how on earth could the firm pay bonuses when it was not even able to pay investors the money they requested?

Cornered, Madoff confessed that everything was lost and that his investment advisory business, the hedge fund, was a fraud and a giant Ponzi scheme. Mark and Andrew immediately informed the judicial authorities and the police.

Two FBI agents, led by Theodore Cacioppi, arrested Bernard Madoff on 11 December 2008 in his luxurious apartment on Park Avenue. The first interrogations started. Madoff remained under house arrest until March 2009, guarded by the police. He had posted a court-approved $10-million bail for this liberty.

Right after the arrest, the FBI raided the head office of Madoff Investment Securities. Their first move was to cut the paper shredder wires. The police investigations were quite time-consuming. Almost all the staff members were ordered to leave the office, with the exception of a few employees assisting the federal detectives.

Following the bankruptcy, most job contracts were terminated and salary payments interrupted. The promised bonuses for 2008 were also left unpaid.

In March 2009, the handcuffed Madoff was taken to a court hearing. At the outset, he had already given up his right to an open trial and a hearing in front of a grand jury. On the spot, he confessed that he was guilty to 11 different crimes. He admitted to everything, including securities fraud, mail fraud, wire fraud, money laundering, making false statements and perjury.

Madoff's request to avoid a large and open trial was perhaps a tactical manoeuvre to avoid having to tell the full story in court, and to try to get a shorter sentence. Or to spare others, including his wife, brother, two sons and other close relatives on the firm's payroll.

Bernard Madoff's sentence was pronounced in June 2009: a record 150 years of jail, theoretically until 2159. However, in view of a recent 20-year reduction of his sentence for good behaviour in jail, the 73-year-old man would be released from jail in 2139, when he would be 201 years old.

One reason for the unusually severe sentence was that, in the view of the court-appointed trustee, Irving Picard, "Madoff had not provided meaningful cooperation and assistance" before his sentencing. On the basis of life span predictions, his lawyers had requested a sentence of 12 years.

The judge, Denny Chin, called the fraud "extraordinarily evil", "unprecedented" and "staggering", and said that the sentence would deter others from committing similar frauds. After the sentence had been passed, one desperate victim, Michael Schwartz, shouted: "I only hope that his jail cell becomes his coffin!"

Madoff was sent to expiate his sins in the Butner Federal Correctional Complex in Butner, North Carolina. It is a resort-style prison, far from his money-hunting grounds on Wall Street and elsewhere.

The investigations continue in various forms, and at least Madoff's auditor, David C. Friehling, and a few other colleagues will still face trials. Friehling has pleaded guilty to securities fraud, investment adviser fraud, making false filings to the SEC and obstructing the IRS.

In October 2009 the trustee sought almost $200 million from Bernard Madoff's brother Peter, his sons Mark and Andrew, and Peter Madoff's daughter, Shana D. Madoff, in a lawsuit. He said that Madoff's family finance business had been "operated as if it were the family piggy bank".

The family members had failed to detect or failed to stop the fraud, and "if they had done their jobs honestly and faithfully, the Madoff Ponzi scheme might never have succeeded or continued for so long". He demanded that they return almost $200 million, to be distributed to cheated investors.

At the end of 2010, several thousand requests for restitution of the invested money, as well as damage claims, had been made to the trustee. Most of those came from smaller investors. Madoff's assets were frozen.

Some investors may also have access to the Securities Investor Protection Corporation (SIPC), a securities industry group formed by the US Congress to help customers of failed brokerage firms. SIPC has $1.7 billion in assets, $1 billion in credit available from the US Treasury and another credit line from several international banks.

SIPC has stated that investors may receive a maximum of $500,000 from SIPC, but only for cash and securities that are missing from their accounts and may be classified as stolen. Indirect investors (for instance, through feeder funds) in the United States were in mid-2010 still not considered eligible for compensation through the SIPC. However, hearings on this issue were scheduled for somewhat later, to consider whether they might qualify for SIPC relief.

Does Madoff Repent?

Does Madoff repent his outrageous crimes?

At least up till now there's little evidence of that. In one sense that's no surprise, as the general attitude of criminals is to try to distance themselves from guilt. Otherwise they fear it would be too hard to live with it.

Instead, we know that most criminals typically blame something else, such as a difficult childhood, bad company, the hard and immoral society, too much temptation, "things going wrong" or that they only tried to help their loved ones, and so on.

But I suspect that Madoff thinks differently. In his mind, he may blame specific people for causing his downfall: inept politicians and their misdirected economic policies contributing to the economic and banking crisis, greedy bankers and insurance executives causing bank failures, weak industrialists, incompetent regulatory agencies who let it all happen and stupid panicking investors.

They were all partly responsible for the worst banking crisis in eight decades. In its wake, the stock market collapse led to his own ruin.

He probably feels that he himself had no bad intentions and that he might have continued, for God knows how long, as an ingenious financial wizard and a good family man – a scapegoat who volunteered to take all the blame on his shoulders and tried to save his family from evil.

Furthermore, like most other fraudsters, he probably disparages his victims and belittles their suffering, perhaps thinking that "many of them made a bundle anyway", "they were all rich" and "stupidity costs".

In January 2009, the unrepentant Madoff still tried to send jewellery worth thousands of dollars, hidden in postal packages, to his friends and children. As these were detected, the police tightened the surveillance on the "Park Avenue Prisoner". After his deceit failed, Madoff was reportedly furious.

Admittedly, Madoff stated in the court hearing in March 2009 that he deeply regretted and was ashamed for his crimes. At the June sentencing Madoff reverted to the same theme: "I made a terrible mistake", "I live in a tormented state", "I couldn't admit that I had failed", "I am painfully aware that I hurt many people" and "I have left a legacy of shame."

These fairly stereotypical statements of regret convey an impression that he tries to belittle his heinous crimes. It is hard to believe that they represented any genuine repentance, but rather, just customary squirming aimed at mitigating the sentence. Possibly his defence lawyer and long-time friend, Ira Sorkin, was behind the mechanical expressions.

Nasty Sociopath?

Madoff clearly has a very split personality. On the one hand intelligent, energetic, pleasant, even charming though slightly withdrawn, and on the other hand, a cold-blooded, smiling swindler, who did not care if he destroyed his friends' and other victims' lives and dreams. In short: a typical sociopath, whose character traits were analysed in chapter 5.

> "It is just incredible that the man could have been such an evil sociopath – that he came into this community, came to the country club, smiled at everybody, shook our hands, greeted us while he knew he was stealing our money," cried a member of the Palm Beach Country Club who lost millions, according to Marc Seal.

Another desperate victim exclaimed that Madoff "stole with his hands and feet".

Stephen Raven, the director of Madoff's London office, regarded him as a pure Jekyll and Hyde case. He did not recognise the person portrayed in the media after the detection although he knew Madoff very well.

Madoff reportedly appeared in a totally different light inside his family circle, compared with his business relations. Professionally he was the discreet "Uncle Bernie", eternally smiling at the world. The family he managed by fear. It was tough love and fear. People were afraid of Madoff as he wielded his influence and threw his bad temper.

A Jekyll and Hyde personality is typical among sociopaths. They behave as the situation demands, in order to get what they want: charming, cunning, strong, lying and cheating to achieve personal gain or enjoyment. They show a total lack of empathy, regret and feeling of guilt, and have a parasitic lifestyle.

Madoff skilfully used the fact that most people are benevolent and full of trust in their fellow beings. He saw the rich people surrounding him only as targets, ready to be exploited without any regrets.

Most people feel a bit of guilt after some minor cheating or lying, an innermost "shame-on-you" reflex. But Madoff was different. He was a compulsive cheater. It was the same to him to whom he lied, or whom he cheated, whether it was his lifelong friend, fellow believer, kind-hearted mentor or family friend such as Levy or Shapiro, a common fool or a charity for cancer victims. All of them were systematically swindled for many years, and apparently without qualms.

Deep despair, repentance and even suicides have followed in Madoff's path. The rich French aristocrat and asset manager, René-Thierry Magon de la Villehuchet, head of Access International, who had invested an amazing $1,400 million of his own and his clients' money into the fund, took his own life in December 2008 – about two weeks after Madoff's arrest.

Unlike Madoff, he could not bear the shame. He swallowed sleeping pills in his office on Manhattan and slashed his arm with a box cutter. In his suicide note he wrote: "If you ruin your friends, your clients, you have to face the consequences."

"If Madoff had a conscience, he would have committed suicide by now," wrote Marie Brenner, a reporter attending the court sessions. His stockbroker son, Mark, was found hanged on 11 December 2010 in an apparent suicide in his Manhattan apartment. Reportedly, he was deeply, deeply angry at what his father had done to him, to everyone. That anger just fed on itself and constantly reopened the wounds.

But the world-record swindler continues to live and can, in the words of the Irish poet William Butler Yeats, continue to "comb grey hair".

THE END

Money has been swindled for at least 2,500 years – for as long as it has existed. The pace has just accelerated as countries have become richer and richer – and swindles more and more global, complex and involving thousands of victims.

The engines of growth for the fraudsters are peoples' everlasting dreams about fast enrichment, their lust for money in our money-focused societies, the gullibility of the victims and the widespread gambling mentality. Money is king.

Personally, I estimate that fraud victims around the world have lost at least several hundreds of billions of dollars in the last decade. The attractiveness of swindling has probably been encouraged by the fact that the related court sentences have generally been lenient (with the exception of Madoff's case), compared with the immense pain inflicted on thousands of hard-hit victims, whose lives and dreams have been shattered.

How Do Pyramids Proceed?

The great money fraudsters' pyramids are satanically ingenious inventions. They appeal to peoples' inherent greed and their hopes of earning big money fast. Their construction is tempting, complicated and opaque enough not to arouse suspicions in the early stages.

The pyramid's various stages generally proceed as follows:

The Pyramid Matrix

Stage 1: Meticulous planning of the pyramid structure and the bait: super-profitable speculation and million-dollar riches on offer.

Stage 2: Silver-tongued bonus-driven sales agents start selling investments, promising quick 15 to 400 per cent profits per year.

Stage 3: Early investors really receive such generous profits, thus serving as excellent references for the next investors that "the scheme works fine".

Stage 4: Rumours about these "piece of cake" profits spread like wildfire.

Stage 5: More generously compensated sales agents are hired to rake in millions, if not billions.

Stage 6: Gradually, suspicions arise among investors, media and authorities. Some alert investors rush to cash in their spoils.

Stage 7: The money inflow peters out, no more profits are paid out, the culprits are arrested or escape, police investigations start.

Stage 8: The pyramid collapses. Investors lose part or all of their stakes.

Not Everybody's A Loser

Swindlers typically try to hide their dirty money in tax havens or through money laundering elsewhere. If caught, part of the loot may be waiting for them after they have expiated their sins. It is not unusual that their money disappears without a trace.

Even if the swindle victims described in this book lost countless millions of dollars, not all pyramid investors were at the losing end. Some of them even gained tidy sums, if they entered the pyramid early and cashed in their profits as long as fresh money still flowed in. For instance, up to one half of Madoff's investors were assumed to have been net winners.

In addition, many sales agents luring investors into the schemes have been on the winning side. The asset management firms and feeder funds have earned hundreds of millions in generous commissions, as confirmed by the Madoff tragedy.

Bad Policy, Bad Banking, Bad Luck – and Bad Supervision

Money and capital markets are dynamic, complicated and unstable. For these reasons their supervision and regulation pose enormous challenges, and their shortcomings facilitate various types of financial frauds, as shown by the SEC's bumbling in the Madoff case.

Historically, in an effort to improve the supervision of the securities markets after the shocking Black Thursday and the Great Depression, President Franklin D. Roosevelt created the SEC and appointed Joseph P. Kennedy, father of President John F. Kennedy, the first chairman of the SEC in 1934.

But for a long time, the SEC's financial and personnel resources and policing capabilities were quite limited. They were principally focused on a fringe of smaller operators, leaving the major established businesses to be managed through "self-regulation" – which created room for financial excesses and recurrent banking crises, actually until this day.

The 1970s saw a lot of soul-searching about the morals of political and business leaders, especially in the United States. But during the Reagan presidency in the 1980s, that process was reversed, with a return towards the old all-American view: "What's good for business is good for the country."

The financial establishment has generally considered that governmental supervisory agencies should not be too strict in applying regulatory measures. In line with that, Reagan's attack on the regulatory system culminated in an executive order requiring a special cost/benefit analysis before any new regulation was put into effect. The goal of this strategy was to reduce "regulatory unreasonableness" and the burden it placed on American business.

Very soon, the deregulation of traditional banking and the securities industry had catastrophic consequences. Obviously, the profits of various freewheeling banks were "privatised", while tax payers had or will have to pay for the appalling losses of mismanaged banks – as witnessed in the recent banking crises.

It was a four-pronged syndrome: bad policy, bad banking, bad luck and, in some cases, bad supervision.

In the early 2000s, an attack on wildcat banking and swindles was launched, following all the lenient years. Among the measures to combat financial crimes were more power to specialised investigation and enforcement agencies, more police resources, bigger budgets, special laws to facilitate prosecution and special courts with judges better trained in dealing with fraud cases.

And, finally, harsher penalties for white-collar crimes both in Europe and the United States, such as Bernard Madoff's extreme jail sentence. Currently, the Washington D.C.-based SEC has a total staff of 3,800 persons, divided into four divisions, 19 offices and 11 regional offices throughout the United States.

In the battle against financial swindles, one untapped resource are the external auditors. Shouldn't these auditors be in a position to blow the whistle if and when they stumble upon serious corporate illegalities or dubious practices?

However, the American Institute of Certified Public Accountants, along with most individual practitioners, for instance, has traditionally held that "the normal audit arrangement is not designed to detect fraud and cannot be relied upon to do so". Individual auditors face a built-in conflict of interest because even if their employer is an independent auditing firm, it is still paid by the more or less reputable corporations they are examining.

An auditing firm that gets a reputation for "overzealousness" in checking corporate illegalities might find itself losing important clients. As one member of a major US auditing firm once stated to James William Coleman:

> "Our responsibility in this connection is to our clients. It does not extend to informing the SEC about immaterial payments if we find them. We are not police for the commission."

Auditors may not be policemen, but they could, it is hoped, help a bit in protecting the public against swindles. Auditors might perhaps even be legally required to report any suspected illegalities to the enforcement agencies in various countries.

Reality Check

Money swindling has been facilitated by smart, smooth-talking and convincing fraudsters, but also by the credulity of many victims. I believe that numerous million-dollar losses could have been averted if the pyramid investors would have posed a few critical questions in line with the reality check that I propose to use if somebody offers abnormally high profits.

The ABC of Reality Checks
- Find out how such princely profits can be made at all (investment mechanisms)
- Ask why other asset managers and banks do not use similar investment methods, if they are so superb
- Find out how the investments and profits are taxed
- Ask who owns the company and find out what their

background is (education, work experience, credit rating, if possible, even any criminal record)
- What professional recommendations can the directors present
- Review the firm's accounts for the last few years
- Find out who the firm's auditor is and check the last audit report (confirm directly with the auditing firm, as audit reports may be falsified)
- Try to analyse how the investment risk can be assessed
- Find out which bank handles the money traffic
- Check that an independent third party is custodian of the invested assets (no self-custody, as in Madoff's case!)

Special warning: If the sales agents are very pushy, insisting that the investment decision is very urgent, beware! Crooks are always in a great hurry since they fear background checks.

Madoff's billion-dollar swindle and many smaller swindles have received a lot of publicity all over the world. The media and malicious people have wallowed in the misery suddenly brought upon impoverished millionaires. For this reason I hope that, at least in the near future, people will be a bit more cautious if, and when, offered such unusually lucrative quick profits.

If somebody were to suddenly propose that they can make a 15-metre (over 49 feet) long jump when the world record is under 9 metres (about 29.5 feet), nobody would believe him. But in the investment world fraudsters time and again present similar fabulous proposals, that instead of a measly 2 or 3 or 4 per cent interest, you can earn 100 per cent or even 400 per cent in a year. Many people fall for it or at least hope that they can cash in the profits early, before the scheme caves in.

Buffett's Lessons

As another reality check, I wish to remind people of the kind of long-term profits the man who is considered the most successful investor in the world can achieve – the respected multibillionaire, Warren Buffett. Over the years, he has generated an over $40-billion asset portfolio, which he, to a large extent, has donated to charities and development aid to poor countries.

Buffett does *not* invest in miracle investment funds offering 100 or 400 per cent profits, or in any hedge funds at that. He is a value investor. He invests in what he believes to be undervalued, successful, stable, easily understandable companies that have a clear and profitable business idea and whose share prices he believes will rise – such as Coca Cola, the huge Wal Mart department store chain, the car insurance company Geico and the Goldman Sachs bank. His cautious approach also means that he never invested in the IT sector because he could not gauge the firms working in it.

Buffett has collected his enormous wealth with an annual return (capital appreciation and dividends) which, on average, has been in the region of 10 to 20 per cent per year. He has been satisfied with such a stable revenue stream because, calculating the compound interest for an annual return of 10 per cent, for instance, means that in 20 years' time an initial capital of €10,000 would rise to €67,300. Nominally the asset would have increased by almost sevenfold.

If not even Buffett has been able to "do better", then it is hardly possible for financially amateurish swindlers.

The Golden Rule in the Swindler's World

In the swindlers' world a lot of people have had to pay for bitter and expensive lessons.

Lax supervision and regulation in many countries' money and capital markets have cost a lot of daring investors dearly and contributed to the international banking crisis starting in 2007. It facilitated frauds such as Madoff's. Maybe there ought to be a sign poster on the most recent worldwide banking crisis stating: "Made in the US."

In the wake of this scandalous crisis in both the US and Europe, the authorities have fortunately started to tighten the supervision of "bungler-banks", suspect investment practices and tax havens. The regulatory strengthening may also be facilitated because financial supervision authorities, banks, asset managers, the media and the general public will probably be a bit more alert in the future if new large market excesses or swindles are suspected.

Also, the fiduciary responsibility of banks and other asset managers in the portfolio investment field in general and in investment counselling will be emphasised – in an effort to avoid such irresponsible behaviour by feeder funds and banks as that seen in the Madoff scam. These generously compensated institutions gladly transmitted tens of billions of dollars of unsuspecting clients' money into Madoff's bottomless pit, without proper due diligence.

But even so, uncertainty and volatility in the securities markets will prevail and perhaps even accelerate. This, as well as increasing prosperity and the everlasting speculative lust of many people, will continue to offer excellent hunting grounds for heartless professional swindlers.

Therefore, keep in mind the real golden rule in investing:

"If it seems too good to be true,
it probably is too good to be true."

References

Abagnale, Frank W. *Catch Me If You Can*. New York, 1980.

Appelbaum, Binyamin, David S. Hilzenrath, Amit R. Paley. "All Just One Big Lie". *Washington Post*, 13 December 2008.

Arends, Brent. "Ruth Faces Living Off A Scant $2.5 million". *The Wall Street Journal*, 29 June 2009.

Arvedlund, Erin. *Madoff. The Man Who Stole $65 Billion*. London, 2009.

BBC Business News. "Madoff Trustee sues HSBC for $9 bn". 6 December 2010.

BBC News. "Fraudster Madoff gets 150 years". 29 June 2009.

Biggs, Barton. "Global Investor. The Affinity Ponzi Scheme". *Newsweek International*, 3 January 2009 edition.

Bjerre, Poul. *Kreuger*. Stockholm, 1932.

Bloomberg. "Madoff Prosecutors Seek to Take Businesses, Loans". 17 March 2009.

Blundell, Nigel. *The World's Greatest Crooks and Conmen*. London, 1982.

Bowker, Lee H. *Women, Crime and the Criminal Justice System*. Lexington, 1978.

Bray, Chad. "Madoff Pleads Guilty to Massive Fraud". *The Wall Street Journal*, 12 March 2009.

Brenner, Marie. "In Court with Bernie Madoff". *Vanity Fair* magazine, March 2009.

Brenner, Marie. "Madoff in Manhattan". *Vanity Fair* magazine, March 2009.

Carswell, John. *The South Sea Bubble Scheme*. London, 1960.

Chancellor, Edward. *Devil Take the Hindmost. A History of Financial Speculation*. London, 2000.

Clapham, Sir John. *The Bank of England: A History*. Cambridge, 1945.

Clarke, Michael, with a chapter by Sally Wheeler. *Business Crime*. Cambridge, 1990.

Coleman, James William. *The Criminal Elite. The Sociology of White Collar Crime*. New York, 1989.

Defoe, Daniel. *The Anatomy of Change-Alley*. London, 1719.

Destefano, Anthony. "Proposals Sought from Brokers for Sale of Madoff Homes". *Newsday*, 14 August 2009.

Deutschmann, C. "Die Gesellschaftliche Macht des Geldes" (The Societal Power of Money). *Leviathan Sonderheft No* 21 (2002):7-18.

Dienst, Jonathan. "Madoff Accountant Set to Make a Deal". *NBC New York*, 30 October 2010.

Dunkling, Leslie & Adrian Room. *The Guinness Book of Money*. London, 1990.

Dunn, Donald. *Ponzi. The Incredible Story*. 2004 (electronic edition).

Efrati, Amir. "Prosecutors Set Sights on Madoff Kin". *The Wall Street Journal*, 11 February 2010.

Efrati, Amir, Robert Frank. "Madoff's Wife Cedes Asset Claim". *The Wall Street Journal*, 28 June 2009.

Feuer, Alan, Christine Haughney. "Standing Accused: A Pillar of Finance and Charity". *The New York Times*, 13 December 2008.

Financial Times. Numerous news reports from 2008–2010, London.

Flynn, John. See reference in Edwin Sutherland's chapter on "White-Collar Criminality" in the book *White-Collar Crime*, edited by Gilbert Geis and Robert F. Meier. New York, 1977.

Ford, Charles V. *Lies! Lies! Lies!* Washington, D.C. 1996.

Galbraith, John Kenneth. *The Affluent Society*. Boston, 1958.

—. *The Age of Uncertainty*. London 1997.

—. *The Great Crash* 1929. Boston, 1954.

Geis, Gilbert and Robert F. Meier. Edited, with Introduction and Notes. *White-Collar Crime. Offences in Business, Politics and the Professions.* New York, 1977.

Gendar, Alison. "Bernie Madoff Baffled by SEC Blunders: Compares Agency's Bumbling Actions to Lt. Colombo". *New York Daily News*, 31 October 2009.

Giddens, Anthony (with the assistance of Simon Griffiths). *Sociology.* 5th edition. Cambridge, 2006.

Glover, Edward, Hermann Mannheim and Emanuel Miller. *Criminology in Transition.* London, 1965.

Goffman, E. "On Cooling the Mark Out: Some Aspects of Adaptation to Failure". *Psychiatry 15* (1952): 451-63.

Gordon, Stuart. *Suuri huijausten kirja* (The great book of hoaxes), in Finnish. Euroword. Espoo, 1999.

Gorton, Gary. "Banking, Panics and Business Cycles". *Oxford Economic Papers.* New Series, Vol. 40, No. 4, December 1988.

Gross, Daniel. "The Money Culture. Membership Has Its Penalties". *Newsweek.* International Edition, 12 January 2009.

Haapasalo, J. "Cleckleyn Psykopaatin Muotokuva Haastattelututkimuksen Valossa" (Cleckley's profile of a psychopath in the light of an interview study). Publication series by the Unit of Psychology, no. 314, University of Jyväskylä, Finland, 1991.

Haapasalo, Jaana (toim.). "Rikollisuuden Psykologiaa" (Psychology of Crime). Publication series by the Unit of Psychology, no. 328, University of Jyväskylä, Finland, 1998.

Hays, Tom, Larry Neumeister, Shlomo Shamir. "Extent of Madoff Fraud Now Estimated at far below $50b". *Associated Press, Haaretz,* 6 March 2009.

Henriques, Diana B. "S.E.C's bumbling 'astonished' Madoff himself". *International Herald Tribune*, 2 November 2009.

Henriques, Diana B. "2 Programmers are charged with helping Madoff hide fraud". *International Herald Tribune*, 14 November 2009.

Herzog, Arthur. "Stalking Robert Vesco". *Fortune* Magazine, 24 November 1986.

Herzog, Arthur. "*Vesco. His Rise, Fall and Flight*". Electron press, 1987.

Hobbs, Dick. "Criminal Collaboration. Youth Gangs, Subcultures, Professional Criminals, and Organized Crime". In the *Oxford Handbook of Criminology*, edited by Mike Maguire, Rod Morgan and Robert Reiner. Oxford 1997.

Howitt, Dennis. *Forensic and Criminal Psychology*. Essex (UK), 2002.

Independent, The. "The Madoff Files: Bernie's Billions". 29 March 2009.

International Herald Tribune. Numerous news articles. 2008–2010.

International Herald Tribune. "Wiesel says Madoff is 'thief' and 'scoundrel'". 28 February 2009.

International Herald Tribune. "Madoff trustee sues UBS for collaboration". 25 November 2010.

Ishmael, Stacy-Marie. "How much money did JP Morgan make on Madoff". *Financial Times*, 26 August 2009.

Jackson, Cecil W. *Business Fairy Tales: Grim Realities of Fictitious Financial Reporting*. Thomson Learning. Mason, Ohio, 2006.

Jaspan, Norman with Hillel Black. *The Thief in the White Collar*. Philadelphia and New York, 1960.

Kafka, Peter. "Rogues, Rubes and Rip-Offs: A Year of Swindles". *Forbes Global*, Vol. 2, No. 12, 14 June 1999.

Kaplan, Thomas. "Going once, going twice: Madoff's boxers". *International Herald Tribune*, 12 November 2010.

Kaustia, Markku. *Essays on Investor Behavior and Psychological Reference Prices*. Helsinki, 2003.

Kindleberger, Charles. *Manias, Panics, and Crashes. A History of Financial Crises*. Fourth Edition. New York, 2000.

Kouwe, Zachery, Peter Edmonston. "Madoff Lawyers Seek Leniency in Sentencing". *The New York Times*, 23 June 2009.

Laitinen, Ahti – Anne Alvesalo. *Talouden varjopuoli* (The Shady Side of the Economy). Poliisin oppikirjasarja (Police publication series), 3/94, Helsinki, 1994.

Laitinen, Ahti. *Vallan rikokset. Oikeussosiologinen tutkimus organisaatiorikollisuudesta ja sen yhteiskunnallisista edellytyksistä* (The Crimes of the Powerful. A Juridical-sociological Study of Organized Crime and its Societal Preconditions). Helsinki, 1989.

Larsen, Egon. *The Deceivers*. John Baker. London, 1966.

Lauerma, Hannu. *Usko, Toivo ja Huijaus* (Trust, hope and swindle). Rohkaisusta johdattelun kautta psykoterroriin. Helsinki, 2006.

Le Figaro Magazine. "Madoff, L'Escroc du Siècle. Les Victimes Francaises Parlent". 21 February 2009.

Lewis, Michael. *PANIC! The Story of Modern Financial Insanity*. London, 2008.

Lieberman, David, Pallawi Gogoi, Theresa Howard, Kevin McCoy, Matt Krantz. "Investors Remain Amazed over Madoff's Sudden Downfall". *USA Today*, 15 December 2008.

Locke, John. *An Essay in Human Understanding*. London, 1690.

Lombroso, Cesare. *L'Homme Criminel*. Paris, 1895.

Lombroso, Cesare & Guglielmo Ferrero. (1896). *The Female Offender*. Fred Othman. Littleton, Colorado, 1980.

MacKay, Charles. *Extraordinary Popular Delusions and the Madness of Crowds*; and Vega, Joseph de la. *Confusión de Confusiones*, edited by Martin S. Fridson. New York: John Wiley and Sons, 1996.

Maguire, Mike, Rod Morgan and Robert Reiner (editors). *The Oxford Handbook of Criminology*. Oxford, 1997.

Margolick, David. "The Madoff Chronicles, Part III: Did the Sons Know". *Vanity Fair* magazine, July 2009.

Markopolos, Harry. *No One Would Listen: A True Financial Thriller*. Hoboken, 2010.

Masters, Brooke. "Trustee accuses Madoff 'soulmate' Kohn". *Financial Times*, 11/12 December 2010.

Mattson, Monika. "Pahanteon Psykologia. Raportti Rikollisuudesta ja Moraalista" (The psychology of evil. A report about crime and morals). Helsinki, 1998.

McCormick, Donald. *Taken for A Ride*. Dorset (UK), 1976.

McCrum, Dan and Anousha Sakoui. "Bankruptcy traders home in on Madoff". *Financial Times*, 18–19 December 2010.

McDonald, John. *Strategy in Poker, Business and War*. New York (1963), 1989.

McLean, Bethany and Peter Elkind. *Enron: The Smartest Guys in the Room. The Amazing Rise and Scandalous Fall of Enron*. Portfolio Trade, 2004.

Melville, Herman. *The Confidence-Man: His Masquerade*. New York, 1857.

Mikkonen, Antti. "Huijaus on tuomittu onnistumaan" (Swindle is bound to succeed). *Talouselämä* magazine, Helsinki, 25 April 2008.

Miller, Arthur. *Death of A Salesman*. Play. New York, 1949.

Minder, Raphael and Diana B. Henriques. "Thousands settle with banks in Madoff case". *International Herald Tribune*, 25 May 2010.

Nars, Kari. *Företagets valutastrategi* (Corporate foreign exchange strategy, in Finnish and Swedish). Helsinki, 1979.

—. (editor and chief contributor). *Excellence in Debt Management*. Euromoney Books, London, 1997.

—. *Raha ja onni* (Money and happiness). In Finnish and Swedish. Helsinki, 2006.

—. *Miten miljoonia huijataan. Suurpetkuttajien värikäs historia* (Swindling millions: The colourful history of great fraudsters). Helsinki, 2009.

Nousiainen, Anu. "WinCapitan pyramidissa huippu oli kapea". (In WinCapita's pyramid the peak was narrow). *Helsingin Sanomat*, 13 December 2009.

Ogunjobi, Timi. *SCAMS – and how to protect yourself from them*. Tee Publishing (UK), 2008.

Palm Beach Daily News. "Bernie Madoff's Arrest Sent Tremors into Palm Beach". 12 December 2008.

Palo, Jorma. *Oravasyndrooma: Rikollista Rahaa Pöyhimässä* (The Treadmill Syndrome: Fluffing Up Criminal Money). Helsinki, 2003.

Pardoe, James. *How Buffett Does It. 24 Simple Investing Strategies from the World's Greatest Value Investor*. New York, 2005.

Penningtvättutredningen. *Bekämpande av penningtvätt* (Committee report on fighting money laundering). Statens offentliga utredningar – Committee report no. 36. Stockholm, 1997.

Pollak, Otto. *Kvinnan som Brottsling* (Woman as Criminal). Stockholm, 1953.

Putwain, David and Aidan Sammons. *Psychology and Crime*. London and New York, 2002.

Ramsland, Katherine. "*The Childhood Psychopath: Bad Seed or Bad Parents*". <crimelibrary.com/criminology/psychopath>.

Raw, Charles, Godfrey Hodgson and Bruce Page. *Do You Sincerely Want to be Rich? The Full Story of Bernard Cornfeld and I.O.S.* New York: Viking Press, 1971.

Reuters. "Madoff Moved to Prison in Atlanta – US Prison Record". 14 July 2009.

Reuters. "Madoff to Appeal Bail, Net Worth Revealed". 13 December 2009.

Safer, Morley. "The Madoff Scam: Meet the Liquidator". *60 Minutes*, CBS News, 27 September 2009.

Samenow, Stanton E. *Inside the Criminal Mind*. Crown, 2004.

Sanderson, Rachel. "Picard's court filing is a blow to UniCredit chief". *Financial Times*, 11–12 December 2010.

Scannell, Kara. "$7.2bn handed to Madoff victims". *Financial Times*, 18–19 December 2010.

Schilit, Howard. *Financial Shenanigans*. Second Edition. New York, 2002.

Schybergsson, Per. *Fördärv och Förvärv* (Acquisition and Destruction). Helsinki, 2007.

Seal, Mark. "Madoff's World". *Vanity Fair* magazine, April 2009.

Searcey, Dionne, Amir Efrati. "Madoff Beaten in Prison: Ponzi Schemer Was Assaulted by Another Inmate in December; Officials Deny Incident". *The Wall Street Journal*, 10 March 2010.

Simmel, Georg. *The Philosophy of Money*. London, 1900.

Smith, Adam. An *Inquiry into the Nature and Causes of the Wealth of Nations*. London, 1776.

Squillari, Eleanor, with Mark Seal. "Hello Madoff". *Vanity Fair* magazine, June 2009.

Steinherr, Alfred. *Derivatives: The Wild Beast of Finance*. New York, 1998.

Sutherland, Edwin H. *The Professional Thief*. Chicago, 1937.

Sutherland, Edwin H. "White-Collar Criminality". In *White-Collar Crime*, edited by Geis and Meier, 1977.

Thunholm, Lars-Erik. *Ivar Kreuger*. Stockholm, 1995.

Wicker, Elmus. *The Banking Panics of the Great Depression*. Cambridge University Press (UK), 1996.

Wicker, Elmus. *Banking Panics of the Gilded Age*. New York, 2000.

Wikipedia, Factual articles in English, French, Finnish and Swedish, 2007–2010.

Wilson, Linus. "Estimating JP Morgan Chase's Profits from the Madoff Deposits". <SSRN.com/abstract> (accessed 23 August 2009).

Yapp, Nick. *Hoaxers and Their Victims*. Robson Books, London, 1992.

Yochelson, S. and S.E. Samenow. *The Criminal Personality, Volume I: A Profile for Change*. Jason Aronson, 2000.

Yochelson, S. and S.E. Samenow. *The Criminal Personality, Volume II: The Change Process*. Jason Aronson, 1995.

Zajac, Andrew, Janet Hook. "Madoff Had Steady Presence in Washington". *Los Angeles Times*, 22 December 2008.

Zelizer, Viviane A. *The Social Meaning of Money*. Princeton, New Jersey, 1997.

About the Author

Dr. Kari Nars is one of the most respected financial experts in Finland. His distinguished career spans various senior banking positions in Washington D.C., London, Paris and Helsinki, including long-time chairman of the Council of Europe Bank. He has been Director International of Finland's central bank, Director of Finance of the Ministry of Finance and Managing Director of the Bank of Helsinki, as well as chairman and member of several corporate boards.

Kari Nars' previous books include *Excellence in Debt Management, Corporate Foreign Exchange Strategy* and *Money and Happiness*. He is a graduate of the University of Helsinki and holds a doctorate from the Swedish School of Economics. He lives in Helsinki and Provence with his wife, and has two children and four grandchildren.